Tax Administration in Theory and Practice

PRAEGER SPECIAL STUDIES IN
INTERNATIONAL ECONOMICS AND DEVELOPMENT

Tax Administration in Theory and Practice

WITH SPECIAL REFERENCE TO CHILE

Norman D. Nowak

PRAEGER PUBLISHERS
New York · Washington · London

The purpose of Praeger Special Studies is to make specialized research in U.S. and international economics and politics available to the academic, business, and government communities. For further information, write to the Special Projects Division, Praeger Publishers, Inc., 111 Fourth Avenue, New York, N.Y. 10003.

PRAEGER PUBLISHERS
111 Fourth Avenue, New York, N.Y. 10003, U.S.A.
5, Cromwell Place, London S.W.7, England

Published in the United States of America in 1970
by Praeger Publishers, Inc.

Library of Congress Catalog Card Number: 72-105414

Printed in the United States of America

PREFACE

This book was written basically for tax administrators and for individuals in the area of economics
and tax policy who must know enough about tax administration to complete the cycle of knowledge in their
own field. The book will also be of interest to tax
lawyers, accountants and tax practitioners in general.
It will give them the general framework within which
their practice operates. This should assist them in
their decision-making process.

In general, each chapter follows the format of
a general discussion of the topic followed by examination of a specific application. Chile, one of
the countries to which the author was adviser in the
modernization of its tax administration, is the specific
example of application used throughout the book.

CONTENTS

vii

ix

LIST OF FIGURES AND TABLES

CHAPTER **1** INTRODUCTION

The tax system of a nation should reflect the social, economic and political aims of the government, and the administrative machinery should be able to implement it equitably and efficiently. As a nation's economic goals expand and its policy objectives change, as its industry grows, diversifies, and shifts geographically, tax policy alters. The administrative machinery must change with it, or the policy changes are not effectuated.

The perpetuation of old thought patterns and bureaucratic inflexibility, combined with gradual, rather than dramatic, change in the economic and social structure, is usually the cause of inadequate tax administration. The tax system shows the signs of strain: tax evasion increases, and administration, if not corrected, progressively deteriorates. This results in a sense of growing injustice felt by the taxpayers, which in turn leads to even greater increases in tax evasion.

If tax administration is effective, policy-makers in government are permitted a wider range of action patterns and combinations. If administration is inadequate, the policy must of itself be inadequate, in that only the less sophisticated alternatives are practically available. If administration is so poor that the evasion rate is extremely high, policy decisions become basically an exercise in futility. The government then must depend on "charitable" contributions rather than on predetermined payments according to an economic plan. Tax administration, therefore, is the key to effective tax policy, rather than the reverse.

In many less-developed countries the lack of capital and the generally paternalistic culture has made government an important factor, if not the most important factor, in the economic development of these countries. Therefore, the need of the government to

3

encourage public-sector savings is greater than that
of governments in the developed countries, since the
availability of private capital is less.

In trying to carry out their role, most developing governments have run aground on the traditional
aversion to payment of taxes. The evasion rate in
many countries runs from 35 percent to possibly 70
percent. This is usually combatted by the passing,
each year, of more and more substantive legislation
to the point where honesty becomes impossible; if all
legal taxes were actually paid, in many cases and in
many countries, the individual or corporation would
pay close to 100 percent tax on income.

One major additional factor is the unwillingness
of the power structure, whatever it may be in each
country, to permit change. This power is invoked not
only against the passage of substantive legislation,
but possibly, even more, for the insurance of bad administration that permits continued evasion of the
laws that have been passed. We may have, therefore,
an impasse where the government, to carry out its
functions, to assist the economy, and to advance the
social welfare of its people, has to resort to borrow-
ing to the limit of its credit. The interest on these
loans eats up more of its revenues and finally causes
an untenable economic position. This may trigger a
change of government but does not alter the basic economic facts of the situation.

An effective tax administration in the hands of
the government becomes a major weapon against chronic
inflation, one of the main causes of economic insta-
bility. It permits the planning boards of all countries not only to plan, but actually to set target
dates years in advance, to achieve major objectives.
With a poor tax administration, this is almost impossible; planning boards are restricted to immediate
objectives, since it is the individual taxpayer--not
the government--who decides the tax intake.

With an effective tax administration, it is the
government which decides which economic sectors will
be assisted and which will not, instead of the individual taxpayer making that decision according to his
ability or willingness to evade.

By freeing the country from the onerous debt which
in time eats up most of the tax intake, an effective
tax administration permits greater independence of

thought and action and increases the national confidence, without which no real forward motion is possible.

It is of great importance to emphasize that the capable and effective tax administration must be neutral. Its job is not to make policy or to make decisions as to who should or should not pay. It is the effective instrument to carry out the decision made by the government in power. Without an effective machine, the policy decisions of each government in power become merely words and noise. This, being recognized by the people, undermines the authority of the government not only in the tax area, which is the more obvious, but also in all other areas.

The way out of this vicious circle is a competent, modern and effective tax administration, which, as its efficiency improves, permits a practical rewriting of the substance of legislation on the basis of the economic good of the country. Such action will foster a moral climate in which each sector to be taxed will pay according to the policy set by the government and at a rate enabling it to pay and continue in business.

Some concomitant points in fiscal policy that are basic to the development of good tax administration are:

1. Clarity and simplicity of the substantive law, worded in order to facilitate administration and to permit broad understanding on the part of the taxpayers. Simplicity makes evasion difficult.
2. The broader the base of personal and corporation income taxes the easier to obtain adequate revenues without allowing the rates to reach such high levels that evasion becomes profitable.
3. Avoidance of an illogical or irrational tax system, an excessive or poorly distributed tax burden, or waste of the revenue collected which gives moral justification to evaders.
4. Any tax reform, to be realistic, must take into account the possibility of obtaining complete and trustworthy information about the object or service being taxed.

Effective administration depends, among other things, on whether the taxpayers can be convinced that (a) the tax is being effectively administered, so that the person who pays, willingly or otherwise, is not being discriminated against, and (b) there is some relation between the payment of taxes and benefits received from public expenditures.

Probably nothing is so detrimental to taxpayer morale than the belief or knowledge that other tax-payers are not being required to carry their part of the load. Tax administrators, then, must maintain an aggressive attitude concerning the correctness of tax-payers' actions. Some taxpayers fail to file or make mistakes through ignorance or neglect; others deliberately cheat. A passive attitude by authorities toward errors and falsifications will soon undermine the entire structure, since the diligent and honest taxpayers will almost in self-defense be forced to the level of the careless and the dishonest.

A tax administration which seeks compliance must protect those who comply--or compliance will diminish. There is a sort of "vicious circle" in which tax administration is adversely affected by the tolerance of the public toward noncompliance, while simultaneously the attitude of the public may be affected by tax administration. The place to break the circle is to improve the administration.

Tax change is a complex and difficult process. Those who specialize in the area of adapting tax systems to the needs of various countries emphasize the need to adapt these systems and policies to the stages of economic development and to the existing institutional setting of any given country.

In discussing the problem of institutional barriers to the application of fiscal policy, Dr. Walter Heller points out that "taxation is itself an instrument of social change. It does not need to wait passively until restrictive and binding social institutions are changed, but can itself help hasten the change." In answer to the argument that those in control of governments will not follow a course of change if it conflicts with their own interests, Dr. Heller cites the growing realization on the part of governing groups that their enlightened self-interest for the longer run lies in the direction of economic development.

CHAPTER **2** THE CHILEAN
CONTEXT

The tax administration of every country must fit
into its basic culture. Since Chile is used as the
example of application throughout the book, it is important that the reader have some idea of the framework
within which the changes had to fit. In addition,
since improvement in tax administration is in great
part measured by diminution of evasion, an idea of results obtained would be of use.

THE COUNTRY

Located at the extreme southwest of South America,
Chile stretches about 2,650 miles along the Pacific
coast, with the high Andes providing most of the
country's eastern frontier. Although it is at no
point wider than 250 miles, Chile (286,396 square
miles) still exceeds the area of many countries. From
north to south, its narrow dimensions are divided into
three zones: the northern desert; the central agricultural area (containing 85 percent of the population);
and the southern forest lands.

The population is predominantly Spanish. The
European character of Chile has been augmented by
heavy immigration, particularly of Germans, Yugoslavs,
and British. There are probably less than 200,000
true Indians in the total population.

Chile is a constitutional democracy operating
under a unitary republican form of government with
legislative, executive, and judicial branches. Its
present constitution, adopted in 1925, grants suffrage
to all literate Chileans over age 21. Voting is by
secret ballot.

The internal economy is dominated by industry and
agriculture, plus a rather remarkable degree of
"services" considering the general level of development.

It has had to rely on exports of nitrate, previously,
and now copper, as well as some agricultural products
for its foreign exchange. Copper is Chile's most important product, and the country ranks third in world
production.

Attempts are being made to diversify Chile's
economy and achieve self-sustaining growth. In the
last two decades primary emphasis has been placed on
industrialization and import substitution. This
harmed the agricultural potential of the economy, and
current development plans call for a better balanced
economy. A conspicuous feature of Chile's economic
history has been recurring inflation which has averaged from 20 to 30 percent per year in the last ten
years.

HISTORY AND CULTURE

Culture is too complex a topic to be analyzed
briefly. However, from a tax-management point of view
it is the frame of reference within which the system
must work.

Chile and most of the west coast of South America
were settled from Peru and for the first 200 years
were ruled by the Viceroy of Peru. The basic culture
of the country developed during that period. This
setting of the basic culture (for some 200 years) in
Peru, with its large Indian semi-slave population,
resulted in the twisting of the inherited semi-medieval
Spanish culture of the times.

In Peru a comparatively few Spaniards ruled a
large conquered Indian population. The situation
fostered a twisted relationship between rulers and
their subjects which has had, over the years, a pro-
found effect on the attitude of the Chilean people
toward their leaders. One of the major problems in
tax administration is the lack of confidence of the
populace in the goodwill of their government.

The Bible tells us that in a master-slave relationship, eventually the slave becomes the master and
the master, the slave. Where there are many slaves
and few masters, the right of decision is a prerogative
of the few and not of the total group, which really
does not expect to participate. The larger group,
therefore, containing people equally as intelligent as
those who make the decisions, shifts, for what a

psychologist would call ego gratification, to a polite
and forced acceptance and a complete mistrust of the
decisions that are made. There results the illogical
situation of the power of decision resting in a few
people, but they are surrounded by so many checks,
restrictions, and general mistrust that there develops
a tremendous rigidity of administrative structure.
The basically defensive system caused by mutual mistrust has come to be a cultural characteristic. Only
within the family group and among "friends" does there
exist a degree of trust that permits definitive action.

        Acceptance of one point of authority leads to a
division between those who command and those who work.
Obviously, when a few command and many obey, working
with one's hands is beneath the dignity of anyone of
consequence, since only the lower class does so.

        Following this type of logic, working with one's
hands indicates that one is an inferior. Carried to
a conclusion in a status-concious culture, the result
has been a division of the population into workers
with little training, a top group of intelligent
trained men, and a small few to bridge the gap between
them and to see to the carrying out of action. In
other words, there is a gap between the leaders of the
community (the thinkers and the trained men) and those
who do the actual work. This results in good, but restricted, planning and very poor or no execution. It
was in this area that much of the tax administration
work had to be concentrated; it was the reason why the
first point of action was the development of a training
school

CLIMATE FOR CHANGE

        The change of such an important segment of a
nation's economy as its tax structure can only come
about if there is a recognition within the nation of
the need for such change. This recognition does not
necessarily have to be that of a majority but can be
of a dedicated and well-informed minority. This recognition of the need for change is not solely in terms
of the nation's economic well-being, as noted in the
Introduction, but also in terms of the political need
for a strong economy that will permit social changes
and greater independence of action for the country
among the community of nations. The hot breath of
involuntary change has in many cases speeded up the
process by creating the feeling that time was of the
essence.

Of some assistance in changing a tax system is the fact that opposition to such change usually comes from both the extreme right and the extreme left. The extreme right opposes change because, in general, its adherents will be the ones making the greatest money contribution; the extreme left opposes it, sometimes even more vehemently than the right, because its take-over depends on chaos and the lack of social advancement. Its members object to the stability and progress permitted by revenue derived from a good tax system.

Another point which assists greatly in change of the tax system is that the watchdogs, both of the right and left, historically have paid the greatest attention to the changes in substantive legislation, although, (in the majority of countries) changes in tax administration are much more important in terms of increasing revenue than substantive legislation. If the changes are planned carefully and put into operation rapidly, there is a tendency for the opposition to be caught napping.

A key factor in putting better administration into effect is the personality and capability of the Director of the Tax Service and the backing he can generate both in the political arena above him and in his staff. Chile was fortunate in having an intelligent, capable, and strong man in the person of Eduardo Urzúa, who had been Secretary of the Treasury in a previous government and who was a man dedicated to the improvement and modernization of his country.

Ultimately, the final success of any change in tax administration depends on the attitude and willingness to accept change and the understanding of the changes by the average inspector and clerk. If these people are represented by a union, and in most cases they are, the backing of the union is of the greatest importance not only in the area of procedures and systems but more important in the attitude and approach with which the systems are used.

At the very beginning of the process of change the key officers of the union were brought into the project in an advisory capacity, their opinions requested and listened to. They became an important factor in the persuasion of the employees of the Tax Service that the changes were for their benefit, as well as for the benefit of the country as a whole.

It is strongly recommended that this be recognized and that the conflict between those who direct

and those who are directed, which is so common in most
countries, be resolved, reconciled, and changed to a
partnership that goes forward for the benefit of all
concerned. This takes a little more time but is para-
mount if a permanent change in mentality and approach
is to be achieved.

RESULTS OF
IMPROVED ADMINISTRATION

The administration of the internal taxes in Chile
is a joint responsibility of the Internal Tax Service
(Dirección General de Impuestos Internos) in the Ministry of Finance (in charge of the assessment function)
and the Treasurer's Office, also in the Ministry of
Finance, which is traditionally responsible for revenue
collection. No real progress in tax administration
could be made unless there was a concerted effort by
both agencies to assess the taxes due properly and
enforce collection at a predictable speed and at
scheduled times.

The changes made to achieve these goals were the
result of long and arduous efforts involving groups as
well as individuals, business contacts as well as
social contacts, internal support as well as external
support. Some were achieved with a minimum of effort
and resistance, others were comparatively more difficult. The long hours of discussion and work have resulted in an organization that is in a position to
move forward with effectiveness in the assessment and
collection of taxes. This in turn has permitted a
change in the substantive law from a policy solely
concerned with tax intake to that of an economically
balanced system.

During the four years of the project, approximately $500 million extra was collected, due, for the
most part, to a better administration of tax laws.
In a country of 8 million people, this is a tremendous
sum that can be used for betterment. We think in terms
of the thousands of houses that can now be built for
people who don't have homes, miles of highways to give
access to areas hitherto untouched, and all other
matters which any government, especially of an underdeveloped country, must do to bring its people into
the 20th Century.

While institutionalization cannot be measured
statistically, the increase in tax assessment by the

FIGURE 1

Additional Assessments by Audit Division,
Internal Revenue Service
(in millions of escudos[a])

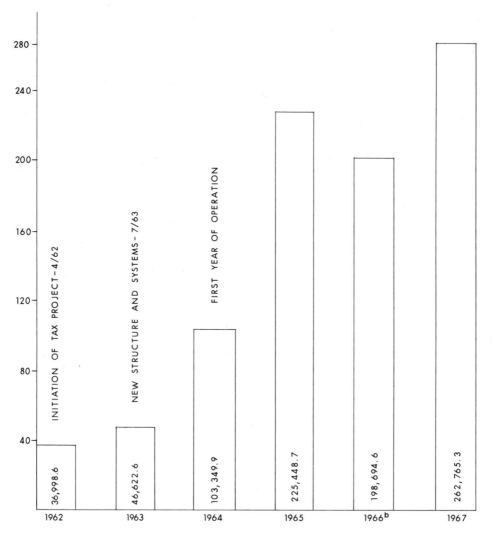

[a]Because of the 3- to 5-year period covered by each audit, the escudos noted are only about 10 per cent less than 1 escudo = $1.

[b]Three months of agents' time was spent on problems other than audit.

FIGURE 2

Tax Intake Through Chilean Tax Service
in Current and Constant Escudos
(in millions of escudos--1 escudo = $1 in 1961)

ESCUDOS IN MILLIONS	1961	1962	1963	1964	1965	1966	1967
		INITIATION OF THE TAX PROJECT APRIL 1962	NEW STRUCTURE INAUGURAT-ED	FIRST FULL YEAR UNDER CHANGES			

1961 VALUE

CURRENT VALUE

13

Audit Division (see Figure 1) in 1967, the issuance
of a yearly work program in 1966 and 1967, and the
generally effective and forward-looking approach the
Tax Service has been taking indicate its progress.
The evaluation of any project depends on two factors:

    1. Its success in reaching the objective--here
an increase in tax intake within a tax structure
reasonably balanced and geared to the economy.
    2. The institutionalization of the changes, that
is, the organization and systems continue to improve
after the advisor has left.

    On the first point, Figure 2 shows the increase
in the tax intake between 1961 and 1967 (in constant
Escudos) or roughly in dollars (1 Eo = $1 in 1961)
from 600 million to almost 1,250 million.

    While the second factor cannot be measured sta-
tistically, progress has continued since the author
left in 1966 and the general belief is that the changes
are fully institutionalized and progressive.

    An analysis of the increase in tax intake and
the institutionalized changes is covered, by functional area, in the chapters that follow.

ESTABLISHMENT OF GOALS

An organizational structure is always developed in terms of its mission or what it is trying to accomplish. The basic mission of all tax services is the development of a climate of compliance (taxpayer conscience) that will cause the taxpayer to either know or make it his business to find out about the tax laws, fill out the appropriate forms, assess himself the correct amount, and voluntarily pay the taxes due. No country in the world can afford an administrative system so large and costly that it could make every taxpayer do the above by force alone.

Basic to the development of this "climate" is the realization by the tax service that the evolution of a "taxpayer conscience" is not a technical matter. The actual money collected by any tax service as a result of technical interpretation of laws, audit of returns per se, decisions by tax lawyers, etc. is a very small part of the total tax take. It is primarily through the creation of a "state of mind" in the taxpaying public that a minimum amount of evasion and a maximum amount of compliance with the law is brought about. None of the techniques of forced compliance per se can be extended to enough taxpayers to have an important direct effect on the tax intake. They contribute to the minimization of evasion primarily by their contribution to the creation of this "state of mind" on the part of the taxpayer which in turn is conducive to voluntary compliance.

In creating this "state of mind" there are many factors outside the control of the tax service, including the following:

1. The realization by the taxpayer that he gets something for his tax money--roads, schools, hospitals, etc.

15

2. A general respect for the government in terms
of the ability and willingness of the government to
carry out all its laws impartially.
3. The economic policy of the government regarding each sector paying its taxes in a reasonable
and just proportion to the rest of the economy.

While these usually are not under its control,
the tax service, as part of its developmental responsibilities, should publicize the favorable attributes.

With regard to those areas within which the Tax
Service has the responsibility for developing a "taxpayer conscience," the most important are:

1. The belief by the public that all taxpayers
comply equally with the law. This is more important
for a proper "tax climate" than the amounts of money
that are paid. Tax reduction by reduction of rates
rather than by evasion is not only good administration, but also sound policy and good politics.
2. The taxpayers' fear of being caught and
punished in the event of evasion. Once an aura of
infallibility in this area can be developed, the voluntary system is on its way to working well.
3. The taxpayers' conviction that the Tax Service
will assist him and make it as easy as possible for
him to comply with the law.
4. A good reputation of the tax service for
technical competence, efficiency and effectiveness in
terms of rapid, accurate and fair decisions.

Bearing in mind the above purposes of tax administration, we have within it two basic, fairly self-
contained functions: (a) the audit function, which
investigates and takes appropriate action to insure
that the taxpayer pays his just share according to the
law, and (b) the collection function, which takes in
and records the payments, sees to it that all returns
are actually filed, and follows up on any payments
that are not made or are made in part-payments according to an agreement with the government. All the other
functions of the tax service--legal, economic, technical, administrative--are services to the above two
functions and must be organized to provide these services in line with the overall objectives.

In developing the organization in line with the
above objectives, basic principles of organizational
structure are used, modified by the habits and customs
of the country within which it must operate.

The development of the organization of the
Chilean Tax Service was approached using accepted
techniques of organizational structure, that is, the
operational level was carefully and clearly delineated
first, in terms of functions needed to achieve the
goals.

It was only after full agreement was reached
on the operations of the Zone Offices that the hier-
archical structure of line supervision and direction
and staff assistance was carefully set up on this
base. This way the levels of administration were
kept to a minimum and the staff functions could be
pin-pointed in terms of the line operation they were
to advise. All the necessary functions involved in
carrying out the objectives of the organization could
then be clearly assigned to a unit of the organization.
This approach avoids the error of assigning functions
to more than one independent unit of the organization
and aids in the identification of the items necessary
and possible to decentralize. By starting with the
operating line and the type of operation, then pro-
ceeding through the actual supervision of the work,
the administrative and advisory services, and finally
the policy areas, the structure can be developed
clearly and completely.

The major decision at the local level, on which
all others hinged, was to separate the actual audit
work (which has the greatest impact on the taxpayer)
from the clerical, technical and information functions.
These, while necessary, have but a minor impact on
the taxpaying public. If this could be done, it would
bring the major function, in terms of purposes, to the
forefront and would put the auxiliary functions to the
background where they belong.

One of the biggest problems in doing this was the
administrative equivalent of Gresham's law of money.
Administratively, it can be stated that "the work that
comes to you tends to drive out the work to which you
must go." As a result, when the specific audit function is mixed up with any other functions in the tax
office, such as technical, clerical or general information, the taxpayer, by being in the office and de-
manding service, does not permit the inspector to go
out and do the basic work for which the tax administrative structure is created--the actual auditing.

THE ORGANIC LAW

In July 1962 the Chilean Tax Service had 26 individual departments or offices reporting to the
Director. There was practically no delegation of
authority, and the cultural and operating practices
did not permit cross-departmental coordination. The
result was a bottleneck in all decision-making and a
very slow tempo of operation. In addition, employees
in the operating offices, receiving no real leadership
or supervision from the national office, or follow-up
on instructions issued, were spending the great majority of their time on paper work. Each office operated
its own paper work system, with the result that little
auditing was being done.

Early in 1962 a law was introduced into the leg-
islature, with the backing of the government, that
laid out a staff and line organization that filled
the needs of Chile (see Figures 3, 4, 5, 6). In
deference to the situation in Chile, the Fraud Division was put under the Chief Counsel since in the
Latin system of justice, the legal and investigation
factors are closer together.

The Training Division, while under Administration,
takes on many of the functions of the Personnel Division: it decides which of the new employees will be
retained, and supervisory promotions cannot be made
unless the individual passes a supervisory course
given by the Training Division.

The Office of Secretary General, common to Latin-
American countries, was left intact and put under the
Administrative Subdirector.

The Planning Division, newly created, brings together electronic data processing, statistics, an
Organization and Methods (O&M) Division, and economic
planning and study, both for tax legislation and audit
programing. This was done because the electronic
machines were being used for statistical studies and
the O&M Division was considered part of the planning
and change function.

The divisions within Operations are the normal
technical divisions, grouped according to type of
tax.

FIGURE 3

Reorganization of the Internal Revenue Service
(Effective July, 1963)

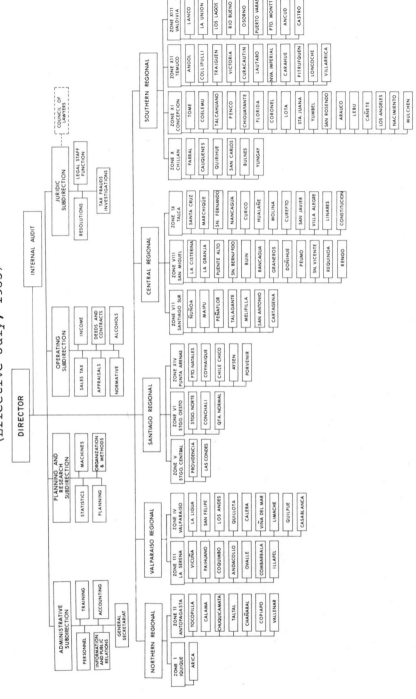

FIGURE 4

Organization of the Internal Revenue Service in Force on June 30, 1963

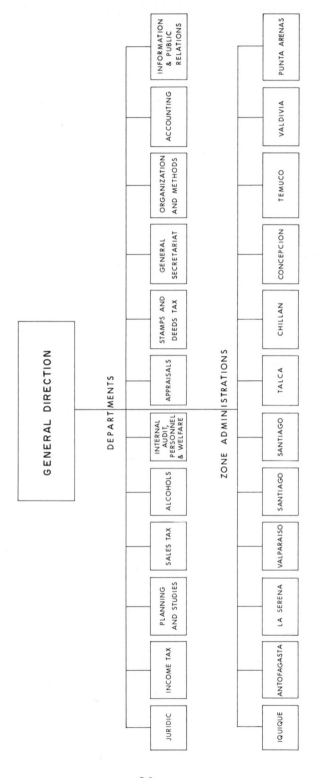

FIGURE 5

Regional Organization

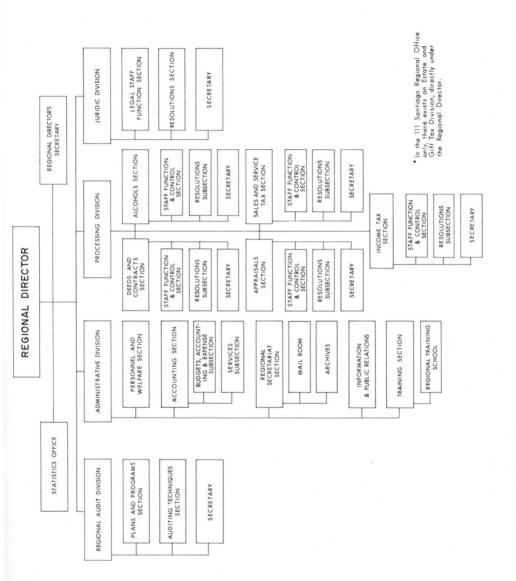

FIGURE 6

District Organization

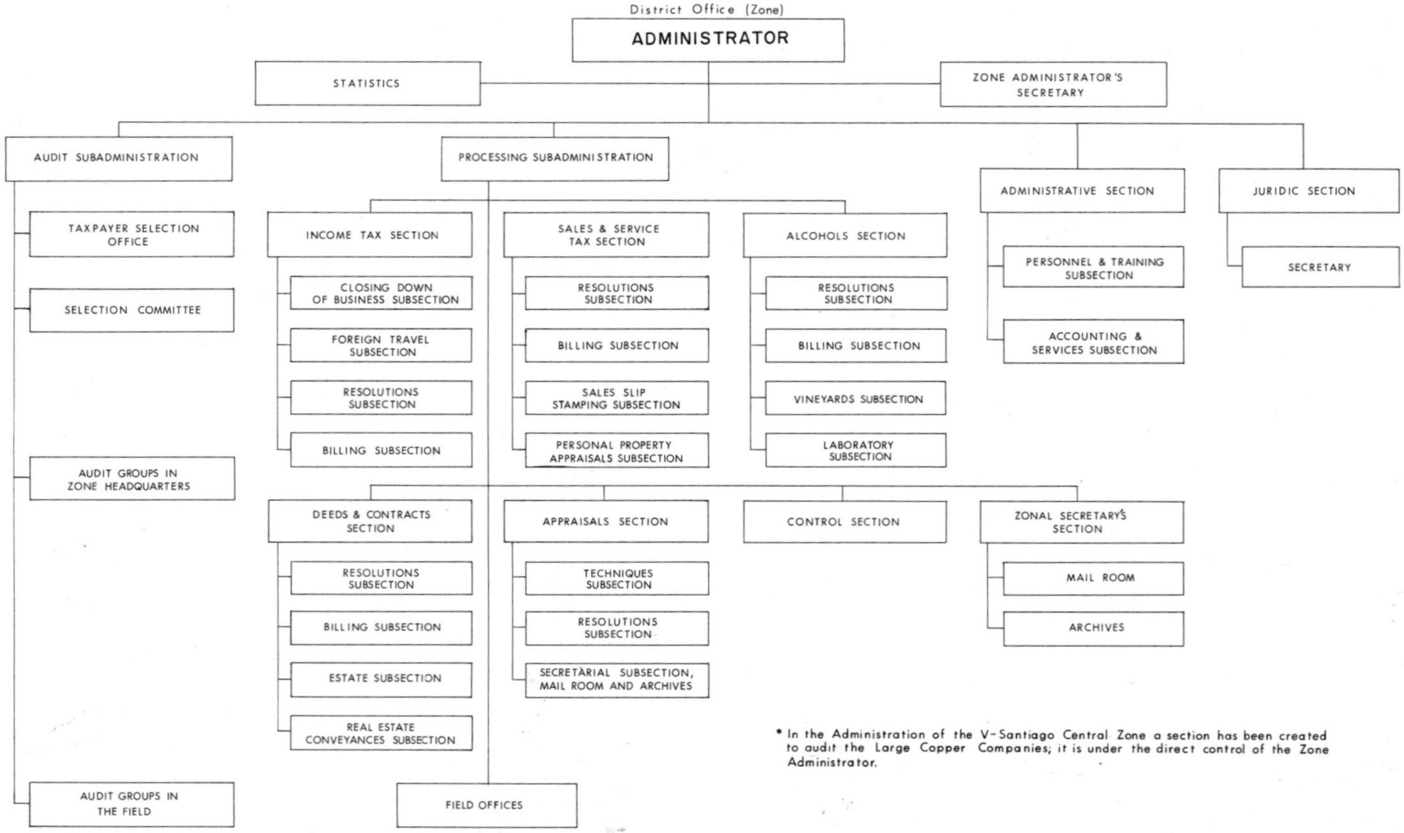

District Office (Zone)

* In the Administration of the V-Santiago Central Zone a section has been created to audit the Large Copper Companies; it is under the direct control of the Zone Administrator.

22

Five regions were established in the country. While only three were really necessary from the point of view of good operation, the fourth came from the specific wish of the government for two regions in Santiago and a fifth region was the desire of the government to improve the services in the North.

The Organic Law laid out only the top structure of the Chilean Tax Service. Even before the law's passage, there arose the necessity of detailing the organization completely.

A Steering Committee consisting of key men, those who would most likely be either subdirectors or regional directors, was established. The author acted as advisor to them. They were given authority to detail the organizational structure and generally to direct all other activities necessary for the change of the organization and systems.

The Organic Law, which passed in December, 1962, provided six months (or until July, 1963) to put the entire reorganization into effect. The first six weeks of work, with the Steering Committee, were the key weeks. During this period the basic changes in the operating levels, the organization of the regions, and the organization and functions of the National Office were decided.

This was indeed a crucial time, because the framework that was going to be established would decide the success or failure of the total change. The basic decision concerned the structure of the operating District Office, because it was that operating structure that, in turn, decided the staff structure of the Regional and National Office.

The new District Office structure clearly separates the auditing from the paper work. Not only is this true at the District level, it is also true in all inspections (branch offices)--no matter how small. Since the revenue agent audits not only Income Tax but also Sales Tax, Transfer Tax and many others, the audit groups were made small (10 or less). At the inspection level the agents report to a Group Supervisor who in turn reports to the Chief of the Audit Division. The paper work is done by a separate division at both the District and Inspection level. (Vol. I of the Manual has complete job and functional descriptions).

Other basic changes were the development of a
planned yearly audit program, classification of returns, assignment of returns by established criteria
to groups and individual agents and development both
of an internal control and a national statistical
system for overall control (Manual Part III and Chapter 4 of this book).

The paper work operation was called "Procesamiento," a word coined by the Steering Committee. Organized basically by the type of tax, procesamiento
is both the clerical operation and the technical court
of the technical adviser to the Zone Administrator on
returns audited by the Audit Division.

In addition to the two main divisions of Audit
and Procesamiento, the Administrator was given a
secretarial section which is called by the old name
of "Secretary General." The head of this function
acted as chief statistician for the office. A lawyer
is also provided as legal advisor. His main work is
in the interpretation of tax law and regulations. As
noted previously the administrative practice of the
country did not permit much cross operation by various individuals on the same organizational level.
This, of course, was something that should change but
will have to change slowly. Divorcing the paper work
from the auditing would force the curtailment of the
paper work, since it became more difficult for the
Audit Division to shift its staff.

One of the major changes made--one which is operating well--was the delegation of authority to take
action in the field. As noted, previously all action
had to be originated at the highest level of the National Office. With systems and policy detailed in
the Manual it was now possible to delegate authority
more or less to the point of action.

Delegation of authority to lower levels without
clear written policy, specific programs and program
goals, and well trained staff is very dangerous,
usually ending in failure. The above three requirements must be met before authority is delegated and
responsibility fixed.

Manual Section 1300 (Appendix A) delineates all
delegations of authority in the Chilean Tax Service
and the point at which action can be taken. In addition this delegation of authority was publicized in the
newspapers and on radio so that the taxpaying public

could demand that action be taken at their point of
contact. The training courses and instructions had
for a full year stressed the point that when authority
has been delegated, the level above would not, even
upon request, make the decision but return the matter
under consideration to the point of delegation.   It
was found that the greatest problem was the acceptance
of authority by people unaccustomed to it.

While the above indicates in general what was
changed, it does not give the background of "how" it
was changed or the climate within which it was
changed.

The installation of a new system can be put into
effect in several ways. One way is to get a small
group of individuals to write up the necessary procedures, methods, organization, and have them signed by
somebody of authority and have them propagated to the
field. This method changes systems and methods but
does not change thought processes or give understanding.

A preferable system is one that brings a maximum
number of staff into the processes of change. The
amount of time necessary for the change is greater
than by the first method, but in the process all key
staff are trained not only in the details but in the
reasons for the changes. In addition, the change becomes theirs, not something ordered from above.

As noted previously, the men on the Steering
Committee were the top men of the agency; those who
would have the key jobs in the new organization. Attached to the Steering Committee were the subgroups
for development of the Manual Communications system,
subgroups for development of procedures and systems
in audit and processing, the programming of training
personnel and the entire ramification of change.
These subcommittees during the first year ranged from
100 to 150 people working directly on the reorganization.

A brief resume of the work of the Steering Committee which directed the changes indicates some of
the methods used.

THE STEERING COMMITTEE--
A CHRONOLOGY

On October 2, 1962, the Director General of the
Chilean Tax Service set up a committee of the chiefs
of the Income Tax, Personnel, Planning, Legal and
Stamp Tax Departments, as well as the Administrator
of the Valparaíso Zone to direct the reorganization
of the Service. This committee was to function as a
Steering Committee, whose purpose was to initiate and
review all work done in this connection. The committee
also was to take all necessary measures for the implementation of the new organization. The following
deadlines were established by them as target dates for
work completion:

Topic	Completion Date
1. Dispatch of Organic Law by Congress	November 1, 1962
2. Passage of Law	December 1, 1962
3. Date of Effectiveness of Law	January 1, 1963
4. Written Instructions on Organization, Functions and Procedures for Service-wide Distribution	February 1, 1963
5. Redistribution of Present Staff and Additional Staff if Necessary	March 1, 1963
6. Housing, Equipment and Facilities, Complete Avail- ability thereof	March 1, 1963
7. Training of all Personnel in New Concepts of Organi- zational Functions and Procedures	May 1, 1963

The work of the committee was of the utmost importance in securing basic agreements and understand-
ings concerning the reorganization of the Service.
The work also involved countless meetings, long and,
in some cases, heated discussions involving key points
and personalities. During the year the committee met
the author had the opportunity to give the committee
members just about the full management course he had
taught previously at the Graduate School of Public
Administration (New York University). The discussion
of each key point was preceded by a brief discussion
of the basic management theory of the point in

question.   The result was a staff trained not only in methods but also in management theory.

In some instances, the work of this committee was delayed through nonattendance by a member, but despite the many difficulties encountered progress continued to be made, though slowly, toward the desired objectives.   Deadlines had to be changed, new target dates were established, and committee membership was altered.   Every attempt was made to continually progress towards full implementation of the reorganization of the Chilean Tax Service.   Some of the difficulties encountered and the number and length of meetings required can be observed from a brief listing of some of the committee meetings.

From October 2nd through 17th, 1962, the committee met regularly.   During this period it presented to the Director recommendations for changes in the Organic Statute that was being considered by the Senate. Specifically, these meetings, whose minutes were kept by a secretary, were concerned with the following:

October 2nd: A discussion of administrative problems resulting from lack of personnel and a discussion concerning the problems involved in the nonpayment of per diem to committee members.   A discussion of a report to be prepared and sent to Zone Administrators concerning the reorganization project.   A discussion of the concept involved in the law that was to bring about the reorganization.   A discussion of the defects in the existing organization due to low salaries, lack of public information, and lack of training.

October 3rd: A discussion of per diem paid to committee members and a request that an attempt be made to obtain additional sums of money for the payment of per diem.   A discussion of the public information program with emphasis on the reorganization of the Service.   A discussion of the meeting dates for the committee and the responsibility of the chairman.

October 4th: The suggestion that a work plan be prepared so that required work be assigned to various members of the committee for completion (accepted). The study and discussion of parts of the proposed Organic Statute covering employee ratings.   The recommendation was also made that employee ratings for the current year be postponed until later in the year. Discussion of the proposed budget to be submitted to the Director.

October 8th: A proposal was submitted for the
distribution and assignment of work among committee
members. This work was divided into functional areas
of responsibility.

October 9th: A discussion of proposed budget
to be presented at the next meeting of the committee.
Continued study and discussion of the proposed Organic Statute. The continued absence of Mr. X was
noted. Consideration of presentation of awards
and bonuses to employees for outstanding work performance. A discussion of the titles to be assigned
to supervisors in the new organization. Discussion
of employee rating. Acknowledgement and discussion
of a note received from Mr. X requesting that he
be relieved from work as a member of the committee
(accepted). Consideration was given by committee
members as to whether a new member should be appointed or if the committee could function without
additional membership.

October 10th: Continuation of the discussion on
the proposed Organic Statute. Continuation of discussion on the awarding of bonuses to employees for
special work performance and a recommendation that
such expenditures be authorized in the proposed Organic Statute.

October 11th: Continuation of the discussion of
work incentives involving a system of employee bonuses.
Members of the committee recommended that Mr. X be
replaced as a member of the committee.

October 16th: A discussion of position classifications and continued discussion on the topic of
work incentives involving prizes and bonuses.

October 17th: Continued discussion of the proposed Organic Statute. Presentation of a plan involving Manual preparation and problems involved. The
Chairman of the Manual Preparation Committee reported
full cooperation from everyone except Mr. X and declared that this failure on the part of Mr. X was
seriously handicapping preparation of the Manual.
After discussion a change was recommended in the proposed organization so that the Fraud Department was
moved from Operations to the Legal Division.

From October 18th through October 31st, the
committee continued to review and discuss provisions

of the new Organic Statute. Recommendations were
presented to the Director for presentation to the
President of the Republic. The committee also reviewed the work done by the six task forces on the
proposed organization functions, delegation of authority, and staffing patterns which were to come into
effect as a result of the new statute. The tax forces
were to be enlarged to include representatives from
each zone of the Service. This change in participation increased representation from all areas of the
Service. A subcommittee was formed to discuss and
develop a training program for the new technical
assistants position that was being created in the new
law. (These were the best clerks, trained for six
weeks, to take over the less technical jobs of the
agents.)

October 18th: Mr. Nowak presented illustrations
of the proposed organization of the Service and explanations of staff and line authority.

October 22nd: Information was presented on the
proposed budget. Several items were insufficient and
required committee consideration. A subcommittee was
appointed to meet with the Director to discuss a solution for the budget problem. Suggestions were approved
for modifications to the Organic Statute.

October 23rd: Discussion of work of the Department of Organization and Methods.

October 24th: Continuation of the study and discussion of the proposed Organic Statute. Clarification of suggestions to be made to the Director regarding sections of the proposed statute.

October 25th: The discussion of the Organic
Statute was completed and the suggestions to be reported to the Director were agreed upon by the committee members.

October 29th: Progress report was made to the
committee regarding the work of the task force committees. Assignments of personnel to prepare written
material for the Manuals were made covering major
areas of organizational responsibility.

October 30th: Agreement was reached on the
schedule of work to be completed and submitted to the
committee for discussion. A further discussion on
the assignment of work topics and responsibilities.

From November 1st through November 15th, the
Senate passed a bill authorizing the President of the
Republic to reorganize the Chilean Tax Service. The
bill was sent to the Chamber of Deputies for consideration. Members of the committee were requested to
attend legislative meetings involving the proposed
Organic Statute so that all recommendations made by
the committee and approved by the Director could be
considered when the Chamber of Deputies considered
the proposed statute. Manual task forces continued to
work toward target dates for completion. Agreement
was reached on the training program to be presented
for the newly created position of Technical Assistants.
Task forces working on organization and functions
completed their reports and were merged with their
Manual counterparts in order to produce final and comprehensive studies and recommendations for the Manual.

November 15th: A report was made to the committee on the functions and responsibilities of the Subdirector of the Legal Division. After discussion the
report was approved. Discussion of the study made on
the Regional Offices resulted in the approval of an
additional Regional Office located at Antofagasta.
Discussion of the report involving the Subdirector,
Administrative Division. Discussions were also conducted on work to be assigned to the Procesamiento and
Audit Divisions. Discussion of the training program
proposed for the Technical Assistants.

From November 16th through November 30th, the
President of Chile informed the Congress that he could
not be bound to a provision in the statute providing
that the top positions in the reorganized Service be
filled according to a strict order of seniority. The
President's position was that these positions should
be filled on the basis of the capability of the individual. The Chief of the Tax Modernization Program
visited several Zone Offices and discussed with key
officials the concept and details of the reorganization. It was recognized in this period that true
tax reform could not be accomplished unless the project was expanded to include reorganization of the
system of collecting delinquent taxes. This involved
meetings with the Legal Collections Division of the
Justice Department. . Plans were also made for a pilot
operation of an Office Audit Group in the Santiago
Office.

November 19th: The committee submitted to the
Director for his consideration the responsibilities

and functions of the Office of the Subdirector of the
Legal Division. Discussion of a report submitted concerning the jurisdiction of regions and zones with
recommendation that the study be submitted to the
Director for his consideration. A discussion of employee rating system submitted to the Director by the
committee for consideration.

November 21st: Recommendation made that in the
future all Monday meetings with the Director be concerned only with topics or material that had previously been discussed and approved by the committee.
Copies were distributed of the committee's report on
the function and responsibilities of the Office of
the Subdirector of Planning. Discussion of this topic
to be conducted at a future date.

November 24th: The Chief of the Tax Modernization Project presented the following topics for the
committee's consideration. These topics had been
discussed with the Director.

1. The Director was to appoint all personnel to
    work on the organization of the Service.
2. The committee would discuss and approve all
    the recommendations involving organization.
3. Geographical distribution of Regional and
    Zone Offices previously presented by the
    committee were approved.

November 29th: The project involving Manual
distribution was presented and discussed.

From December 1st through 15th, the Congress
accepted the item veto exercised by the President.
This empowered the President to appoint key officials
according to capability rather than seniority. Meetings were held concerning the reassessment of property
taxes throughout Chile.

December 5th: Preparation and distribution of
the Manual was approved in accordance with the report
submitted by Mr. Nicklas (Tax Advisor). The jurisdiction of Regional and Zone Offices was presented,
discussed, and approved.

December 12th: Request made that committee
meetings be held on time and according to schedule.
Report made on the study program concerning Technical
Assistants.

December 13th: Discussion of committee assignments concerning the organization of the National
Office, the Regional Offices and the Zone Administrations. Discussion of a report on delegation of
authority.

Between January 1st and January 11th, 1963, the
regulations for the new Organic Law Statutes were
completed. Final review was conducted on new auditing
procedures which were to form part of the Manual volume on audit.

January 7th: Discussion regarding the completion
of work on the following topics: (a) Organic Statute;
(b) Tax Code Modifications; and (c) Employee Rating
System. The Director stressed the urgency of comple-
ting work on these assignments. Work committees were
organized for this purpose. Facilities management
was notified to begin plans for Regional Office locations and furnishings.

From January 11th through 31st, routine work continued to occupy the attention of the committee.

January 22nd: Suggested deadlines for work completion were presented. After discussion the following dates were agreed upon:

Topic	Date Due
The Organic Statute	Ready
Employee Rating	January 29th 1963
Tax Code	January 23rd. 1963
Procesamiento	January 24th, 1963
Auditing -- Structure	January 25th, 1963
Delegation of Authority	January 28th, 1963
Planning	January 31st, 1963
Administration	February 1st, 1963
Legal	February 4th, 1963
Auditing -- Systems Offices, Field and Preventive	February 5th, 1963
Training	February 8th, 1963

From February 1st through May 31st, work continued despite the vacation period and the need for
employees to avail themselves of a much-needed period
of relaxation and rest. During this period a pilot
operation was established in the Santiago Office involving an Office Audit Group using methods that were
to be established within the new organization. A
substantive tax reform bill was under study by the
Congress with passage expected by mid-year.

February 2nd: Discussion of employee ratings.
The committee set preliminary work standards for the
audit function.

February 11th: The committee approved amendments
to the Tax Code. Discussion concerning the responsibility of the Regional Auditing Division and the auditing function at the zone level. The committee
approved the report on the organization and functions
of the Subdirector, Planning and Administration.

February 21st: Discussion as to target date for
completion of the Manual. Need for urgency was
stressed because the committee's pending work had to
be reflected in the Manual. Discussion of the staff
training program and the adequate preparation of staff
members for the new organization.

March 5th: Progress reports were discussed on
facilities management and auditing procedures. Discussion also conducted concerning a review of the
Audit Manual by outside authorities such as accounting
or legal firms. (Price-Waterhouse reviewed the technical park of the Manual.)

April 3rd: Discussion of the preparation of the
Manual.

May 30th: A status report prepared and discussed
on a list of work projects that the committee had
studied and approved.

From June 1st through June 30th, 1963, the first
volume of the Internal Tax Service Manual reached
completion. A training program for the new organization was scheduled so that all employees of the Service could be trained in the concepts and procedures
involved in the new organization. A delay in the appointment of personnel in the 3rd through 6th catego-
ries cause problems with the new reorganization.

June 4th: Discussion of regional jurisdiction.
An amendment of the resolution of December 5, 1962,
gave the Santiago regions a new structure.

June 10th: Discussion of the distribution of
personnel. The definite assignment of personnel was
agreed upon at successive meetings.

From July 1st through October 31st, the reorganization of the Chilean Tax Service became a reality.

Complete efforts of all personnel were directed at
this time to the physical organization of all functions
of the Service. Meetings of the committee were conducted at irregular intervals and only when necessary
for the purpose of discussing emergency measures.
Teams consisting of one advisor and three staff members fully conversant with the concepts and details
of the reorganization were detailed to the Regional
Commissioners for the first month of the reorganization to help them put it into practice.

September 5th: Discussion of the Annual Auditing
Plan for 1964. The Director requested that the
Visitador General (Inspector General) establish a
visitation schedule that would coincide with the Annual Auditing Program. A discussion concerning attempts of the employee groups to obtain salary
increases. The request for overtime work by the employees for the remaining four months of the calendar
year was denied by the Director on the grounds that
the need for such overtime work had not been proven.
Discussion of the need for internal information on
the responsibilities of the various departments or
divisions so as to expedite decentralization and to
provide better use of telephone communications. Concern was expressed by the Director over the activities
of the Santiago Region. A task force was organized
consisting of all the Subdirectors and the Visitador
General (Inspector General), for the purpose of making
a study of the organization of the Santiago Region.
A discussion of the establishment of a library within
the Subdirector Legal Division. It was decided that
the Training School Library would remain as a Central
Library for all functions within the Service. It was
agreed to delay the press conference regarding the reorganization until there was reasonable assurance that
there was a minimum of complaints or criticism from
the public.

October 3rd: Discussion of the building located
at Bandera and Agustinas as a possible location for
the Santiago Region. The Regional Director of the
Santiago Region stated there were not enough lawyers
assigned to his Regional Office. Discussion was also
conducted concerning location of the Inheritance Tax
Section. The Subdirector Operations reported that the
Procesamiento Division in the Santiago Region was not
operating in accordance with the Manual and that employees of this region were not following Manual procedures. A group of Visitadores (Internal Inspection)
was assigned to investigate the situation by the

Visitador General (Inspector General). The Regional
Director of the Centro Region reported by comparison
that his region was functioning in accordance with the
Manual procedures and that they were experiencing no
inconvenience. The Regional Director for the Santiago Region, was quoted as expressing the opinion
that the reorganization was not in accordance with the
reality of the Chilean situation. He claimed that
he referred only to the procesamiento part of the
organization. The Director advised the Regional
Director to follow procedures. It was recommended
that a study be made of the procesamiento part
of the Manual and that there be a further discussion
of the duties of the Chief of Procesamiento with a
view to studying the position for possible revision
of the functions. The Director expressed his confidence in the organization and asked for full cooperation from the part of all employees and supervisors.
He requested that all make their best efforts and try
to make the organization a success.

October 10th: Discussion of the purposes of the
Visitadores (Internal Inspection) function and their
responsibilities, including clarification of the
meaning and methods of internal audit. Discussion of
the field audit function in auditing. The need for a
professional staff of accountants capable of going
into the field and making all types of audit.

On April 27, 1964, the Regional Director of the
Santiago Region was relieved of his major zone,
the fifth zone referred to as Santiago Central.
This zone was reorganized according to instructions prepared by a committee consisting of the
Subdirectors, Administration, Planning, Operations
and Legal, and the Visitador General (Inspector
General). The Chief of the Tax Modernization Project
acted in an advisory position to this committee.

One of the major accomplishments achieved by the
formation of the Steering Committee was that the men
who became the Subdirectors and key Regional Directors
were given almost a full year of training in the concepts of organization and management as specifically
applied to the Chilean Tax Service. In practically
every meeting, as a problem developed, the advisor
and the group discussed the general organizational
and management principle upon which the decision would
depend. As a result, the top echelon of the Service

not only knew the total structure of the reorganization thoroughly, but also knew the "WHY" of the new
organization.

There have been several critical reviews of the
actual operations of the structure to date; however,
very few changes have been made. The only changes
have been that the handling of inheritance taxes and
appeals has been centralized at the regional level
and the smaller branch offices (2-3 men) consolidated
under an inspector.

CHAPTER **4** TAX SERVICE
MANAGEMENT
TRAINING

A technically oriented tax agency has great difficulty in the acceptance of modern management principles. Especially difficult is the concept that a
"manager is a person who makes things happen through
the efforts of others." The type of retraining necessary to substitute new habits for old, ingrained ones
is most difficult and time consuming.

ELEMENTS OF SUPERVISION

It is an accepted principle that in making management changes one must start at the top. Only as
the executive staff understands and accepts the basic
concepts can training situations and new techniques
assist, gradually, in transferring change to the lower
levels of supervision.

All of the training centered around the following
eight basic requirements of supervision.

1. What is to be done? This question concerns
the planning of objectives and the defining of specific goals to be reached by a projected operation. It
is here that the broad aspects of workload are deter-
mined--how much of what will be done.
2. How will the work be divided? This question
relates to the problem of manpower use and proper assignment of responsibility and authority to enable
all the organizational elements to function effectively. Proper answers are reflected in result-pro-
ducing organizations.
3. How will the work be done? This question is
concerned with methods and techniques to be used in
performing assigned tasks. It deals with policies and
procedures which will govern the operation, both those
in existence and those to be developed.

37

4. Who will do the work? This question covers
the area of personnel actually involved in doing the
work and includes consideration of qualifications and
skills of individual workers in the light of their
contribution to the overall program. It concerns the
requirement, availability, training, classification,
assignment, and use of personnel.

5. What will the work be done with? This question deals with the facilities, material, and money
required and available to carry out the projected
work.

6. When will the work be done? This question
covers the area of proper placement of the assigned
task in the time schedule of all related tasks and
includes establishment of priorities for the different
elements of the task.

7. How well should the work be done? This question covers the determining of standards of quality
of performance and of end results to enable comparison
of actual with expected performance.

8. How well is the work being done? This question involves the appraisal of results in terms of the
meeting of standards, correspondence with the planned
goals, the meeting of established time schedules, and
contribution to overall effectiveness.

PRELIMINARY MANAGEMENT TRAINING

Training Abroad

As any pedagogue knows, training, to be successful, not only must be used immediately but also should
appeal to as many of the senses as possible. Teaching
by lecturing is extremely useful and usually the easiest way. But it is much more effective, if possible,
to permit key people in the organization to actually
see how some of the concepts they have heard of are
operating. Using this approach, every key supervisor
(down to Zone Administrators and the Division Chiefs
at the National Office level in all cases, and below
that level as warranted) were sent to the United
States to observe, in their functional area, how
similar procedures and approaches were actually working. During the four years of the project, well over
one hundred staff members received this training in
every one of the functional areas.

The contact they had, the knowledge they acquired,
and more important, the feeling that progressive change
was possible, became part of their consciousness. This

was of major importance in putting the changes into
actual operation. The only possible contrary argument on many of the key points of change was the possibility that "this could be done in the United States
and nowhere else." This was a poor argument for a
proud or intelligent man to use. The numbers of people sent had a positive effect on the entire organization, and since the people selected represented
many regions of the country, this attitude permeated
the entire structure.

It is suggested, based on this experience, that
this type of learning by seeing and observing be
carefully planned and the area under study be as narrow as possible. The least effect was accomplished
by tours to look at everything. The greatest effect
was due to observational training in a narrow functional area that covered all the details of operational theory and methods. A concomitant point is
that, as much as possible, a minimum amount of
training should be in a classroom situation and a
maximum should be observation.

Seminars and Training Sessions

As noted previously, the Steering Committee,
which consisted of the key executives of the tax organization, did in essence attend a one-year seminar
during the process of the development of the entire
structure. The benefits of this were invaluable. In
addition, during the process of change, a series of
seminars explaining organizational and supervisory
concepts, their use in the new structure, theory of
communications, etc., lasting from one day to one
week, was given to all members of the Tax Service,
from the Director to the lowest-level file clerks.
This was achieved by starting with the one-week seminar for the Director and all key staff, including the
Steering Committee members, assigning these individuals to the Regional Offices where they ran similar
seminars for key executives of the Regional Offices,
and then in turn to the Zone Offices and down to the
smallest districts. At each stage, personnel from the
ranks above were present to assist and advise.

In addition, seminars on work simplification and
other management topics directly connected with the
structural changes were held for management staff
during this four-year period in order to continue their
education and increase their consciousness of the need
for improvement.

Chilean-American
Philosophical Society

Late in 1962, the Chilean-American Philosophical
Society was founded. The meetings, held in the evening at the author's home, were attended by 35 to 40
of the top men of the Chilean Tax Service. In addition
there usually were representatives of the Treasury and
the Office of the Treasurer. At typical meetings,
mimeographed copies of an article of between 3 and 5
pages on a pertinent management topic were distributed to those in attendance. For an hour and a half
there would be a round-table discussion on the subject
in question. (See Appendix C for a list of topics
covered.) These discussions usually became quite
animated, especially as the points in discussion were
applied to the operations of the Tax Service. After
the seminar was officially recessed, small groups of
interested members continued the discussions--often
for several hours.

The meetings also served a secondary purpose.
Since the Director and the Subdirectors were present,
the meetings tended to become a council of all key
supervisors, where the management point under discussion was tied into the operations of the Service.
Other pertinent problems were openly discussed in an
informal manner and agreements were reached. The
author considered these meetings, held over a period
of three years, one of the most important tools for
developing good supervision and management within the
Service.

Supervisory Training

The first course developed after the course on
"How to Teach" was a course on Supervisory Training.
This was developed for first-line supervisors and ran
from 6 to 8 weeks. It consisted of specifics for both
audit and procesamiento supervisors that not only gave
the theory of supervision but also brought it down to
the practical level. A resolution issued by the Director stated that this course was mandatory for all
supervisors and that no man could be promoted to a
supervisory position without taking the course and
passing an examination on it.

In addition to promoting knowledge and the ability to carry out jobs in a more forceful and positive
manner, the Supervisory Training Course brought new

ideas into all offices. The fact that it was mandatory for promotion to supervisor stressed the importance of this knowledge to the Tax Service personnel.

CHAPTER **5** STAFF TRAINING

The author's first activity to achieve staff
training was the establishment of a training school
in the Internal Tax Service. The resons for this
included the following:

1. The educational background and lack of
previous training in the Service of most of the
staff.
2. The great hunger for education in South
America a school meets less opposition than any other
suggested change.
3. The establishment and organization of a
school does not take a great deal of time (2 1/2
months in Chile) and permits a good start with a
popular change.

Most studies on reorganization agree that training seems to be a "sine qua non" and that the establishment of a training school with an adequate course
of study would possibly produce the desired results.
Training can accomplish many things, but training by
itself is not capable of creating miracles.

To prepare training courses of study with no
improvement in work situations is a virtual waste of
time. On the other hand, it is the sort of thing on
which the Chilean people, with their desire for knowledge, would all agree. It is acceptable to attend
school, to discuss theories of taxation, to improve
one's knowledge of tax laws, to become familiar with
modern techniques of instruction, and to analyze the
strengths and weaknesses of an organization.

But this training is of no use if the people,
after having been trained, lack the discipline, authority, or opportunity to take the material studied
and put it to effective use. Training is of little
use if decision-making is retained at the top level,
so that subordinates cannot put into practice

knowledge acquired in the classroom. The training
would be usable only if followed swiftly by reorganization.

THE TRAINING SCHOOL

In setting up an in-service training school the
first, and usually major, problem is space, then (in
order of difficulty) furniture, course outlines,
teachers, and finally students.

Regarding the problem of space, one of the main
problems of any school, we were fortunate. A new
addition to the Treasury Department was just being
completed and I was assigned a corner office on the
same floor as the Director before the building was
occupied. Taking advantage of the natural politeness
and great interest of the Chileans by placing a few
pieces of furniture in the various rooms of the new
building (the new school) I acquired two floors; ample,
new and well lighted.

With the space assured, teachers, furniture and
course outlines were now needed. The Director was
able to secure $50,000 for the furniture. Diliberate-
ly, light blonde, Swedish modern furniture was bought
to indicate visually the departure from the old system
where the heavy, dark, Spanish type furniture was used.
It took about six weeks to have the furniture made to
order, during which interval a substantial amount of
time was spent arguing the acquisition of this type
of furniture before the Central Purchasing Committee
of the government. All new things take time and
patience to approve and I would like to acknowledge
a debt to those people who took a chance on this new
type of furniture for the government. I would digress
here and note that on my return to Chile some 10
months later, the same type of furniture was being
purchased by the Central Purchasing Committee for the
rest of the government and they had set up an exhibit
in their offices for other government agencies to see.
The head of the Central Purchasing Committee had also
refurnished his office the same way.

The problem of obtaining teachers for the school
was both easy and difficult. There were many intelligent, well-trained men in the Service who also were
instructors at various universities and secondary
schools. The method of teaching, however, was the
old: "lecture and regurgitation." The effectiveness

of this system is doubtful in most disciplines; it is
useless for in-service training. In addition, formal
training outlines were not used.

Since the school needed about 40 instructors for
our first group of classes and since course outlines
for several courses had to be written, it was impossible for one person to guide this. To assist,
therefore, on the training of the instructors and the
writing of the course outlines a Management Consulting
Service, which was part of the University of Chile,
was hired by the Internal Revenue Service and it was
a tremendous help in handling these two phases of the
work. No one was permitted to teach until he had
passed the courses on "How to Teach" under a case
study, student-oriented system.

During the months of August and September there
were approximately 100 of the best people of the
Service working in groups on the course outlines.
The school itself, complete with trained professors,
course outlines for both students and instructors,
and furniture, was initiated in the middle of September 1961 in a ceremony attended by the Secretary of
the Treasury and all of the key men of the Tax Service. It has been continued and amplified to this
day and is now recognized as an international training school in tax administration for South America.

Before we leave this part of the training chapter,
I would note an interesting side fact. As noted
previously, many of our instructors, then and later,
taught at secondary schools and universities. They
brought back to their classes at the university the
student-oriented case study method of teaching.
Other professors came to listen to this technique
and I understand the new method of teaching has
slowly spread and made an impact upon the teaching
techniques of the other professors at the university.

The Training Department was to play a major part
in the reorganization of the Service. Its responsibility included the establishment of training schools,
the development of training materials, the preparation of instructors capable of using the materials,
the screening of all new staff hired for the Service,
and the final decision on retention in the Service of
all new staff.

Initially, about 90-100 staff members were employed in the development of training courses. These people were used either as consultants in determining what material should be included and in what courses, or they were used to actually write the training material for presentation in the training schools.

Three training schools were established: Santiago in September 1961 and Valparaíso and Concepción in September 1962. Santiago, of course, is the largest of the three, with the most adequate facilities for training. All three schools are equipped with modern furnishings, symbolically and deliberately to represent a clear break with the old tradition.

There were three minor but important problems during the initiation of the school and during the first 2 to 3 weeks.

First the agreement that classroom training must be full-time and not on a 1 to 2 hour a day basis. Without agreement on this point, which was difficult to get, the entire base of the school would have dissolved. Second, the old habit of coming late to class. The first week students wandered in up to an hour late. Despite yells of "you can't do it" a rule was made and adhered to that all classroom doors are locked 5 minutes after the start of the class. In two days the problem disappeared. Third, some instructors objected to using the new system of in-service training, case-study method. The resignation as a teacher of the one most vocal was accepted before being offered.

The reaction of the students to the new system made it difficult in a short time to use any other method. This was helped by the fact that the classrooms, deliberately, were made to hold no more than 25 students.

TYPES OF TRAINING

The first efforts of the Training Department were concentrated on providing training for all revenue agents. This training covered such topics as technical tax laws, accounting, auditing, employees' rights and privileges, public relations, and work planning and programming. The initial course, referred to as the first phase of Inspector's Training, consisted of

166 sessions of 1 1/2 hours each. All inspectors were
required to complete this course. The second phase
consisted of 190 sessions of 1 1/2 hours each. Much
of the material contained in the initial courses for
inspectors was based on what Training Council members
thought inspectors should know rather than what was
actually needed by these inspectors to fulfill their
functions in the administration of the tax laws. For
example, not all inspectors are employed in the review
of tax forms. The payroll title "inspector" does not
always mean that a person will actually audit the
books of a taxpayer. In some cases an inspector may
be a lawyer who is appointed for legal work involved
in auditing, or an engineer whose professional knowledge is needed in some areas of tax administration.
Therefore, not all inspectors needed a complete course
as planned and presented. Nevertheless, all inspectors initially were required to take the inspector's
course.

Those who successfully completed the first phase
were permitted to enroll in the second phase. Those
who did not complete the second phase were not appointed to the position of field agent but rather remained as office auditors or as canvassing inspectors.

The reasoning advanced for the requirement that
all inspectors be required to complete an inspector's
course involved an understanding of the educational
background and experience of the inspector corps.
Many inspectors were found reasonably qualified to
perform the duties required in auditing a taxpayer's
return. There was an equally large number, however,
who lacked a basic knowledge of accounting and auditing procedures.

The decision to require all inspectors to com-
lete the inspectors' training course presumed that
upon the completion of training the Internal Tax
Service could be relatively sure that all field inspectors had substantially the same basic tax and
accounting knowledge.

Other training provided in the first year by the
Training Department involved supervisory training for
Inspector Group Chiefs and instructor training for a
selected group of trainees. Courses were given in
supervision to those people who were expected to be
named supervisors when the decree was finally approved
establishing the new organization of the Service.

From the period January 1 through June 3, 1963,
most of the plans for training were made as preparation for the establishment of the new Training Department as of July 1, 1963. This transitional period was
not without problems, including the very complicated
change in administrative authority and personnel
within the Training Department.

Despite this administrative uncertainty, progress
continued to be made. A course for property apprai-
sers was prepared and given. This course was required
for new personnel who were appointed to assist in the
nation-wide project of reassessment of all properties
in Chile during the next two-year period. Additional
courses for inspectors were given by the training
school. These courses were revisions of the courses
given in calendar year 1962. More emphasis was placed
on student participation and case problems.

In order to permit inspectors to be free of office work and devote full time to auditing, a job
called Technical Assistant (Técnico Ayudante) was
created. The people selected for this job were the
best and most experienced clerks who then were given
a 3-month training course on their new job.

A training course was prepared for these people
and approximately 250 employees were trained as Technical Assistants.

When it developed that some Technical Assistants
would not be assigned to the field but would be retained in administrative positions, such as administrative assistants to Division Chiefs, etc., a special
course was prepared to meet the needs of this group.
This course was referred to as Course for Technical
Assistants (Secretarial).

An attempt was made to provide some training for
typists and secretaries. Because of the limitation
of personnel in the Training Department, and the press
of other priority programs, only one course of four
months was given in each of these clerical areas.

The great push forward in quality of training
provided coincided with the arrival of Al Architzal,
the training advisor in 1963. A very competent and
dedicated person, he left his imprint on the entire
structure of the school.

His arrival coincided with the new organization
of the Internal Tax Service which came into being on
July 1, 1963. To thoroughly familiarize all employees
with the concepts of the new organization, their responsibilities, and the functions of personnel at
varying levels within the organization, a training
program was prepared for presentation throughout the
entire country. All employees from the Director at
the top of the organization to the clerk at the bottom
of the organizational structure were scheduled to
participate in training concerning the new organizational structure. A total of 2,379 employees participated in these training sessions that extended from
Avica in the north to the Strait of Magellan in the
south.

The training progressed by stages. The first
training was provided through seminars for the Director, Subdirectors, and Regional Directors. The second
level of training involved Zone Administrators, Chiefs
of National Office Departments and Regional Division
Chiefs. The third level involved Zone Division Chiefs
and Group Chiefs in the Auditing Division. Subsequently, all other employees were scheduled for
training. The last group to be trained were the Internal Auditors. Following this training session Internal Auditors were assigned and sent into the field
to determine whether procedures were being followed.

To assist in this training and in the organization of the regions, five teams of advisors were established. Each team included a member of the
advisory staff who acted as coordinator for the team's
efforts. The teams consisted of specialists from the
Internal Tax Service in the areas of audit, processing,
and administration. These teams stayed in the region
to which they were assigned for the first one to two
months of the reorganization, depending upon the size
of the region and the problems encountered.

Training of instructors in modern methods was a
continuing major problem for the Training Department.
While some efforts had been made to train an instructor staff through the use of the Technical Cooperation
Service, results were not completely satisfactory.
Therefore, it was decided to press forward as rapidly
as possible with the development of a course for instructors that could be used by the Training Department in the training of instructors. This course,
Training No. 1, entitled Instructor Training Program,
was issued by the Training Department in 1964.

Training of supervisors assumed a priority position in the Training Department's plans. The Organic Statute that established the new organization required that all supervisors complete and pass a course of training in fundamentals of supervision. In addition, before a person could be appointed to a supervisory position, he must also have completed and passed such a course. Initially, a training course was prepared for all incumbent supervisors. The course, while practical, did not fully meet the needs of new supervisors. Training No. 2: Fundamentals of Supervision, was prepared and is now being used by the Training Department.

Some positions in the new organization were new in concept and in responsibilities. The position of Chief, Administrative Division, was such a position. The employees appointed in July found that they were in difficulty. They had trouble in determining exactly what their functions were and how they could demonstrate a need for their services. In October 1963, to fulfill this need for training, a one-week seminar was conducted at the National Office Training School for all Regional and Zone Chiefs of Administration. Throughout the week classes were conducted to teach the various administrative responsibilities and attempts were made to demonstrate how these responsibilities could be met by the Chiefs of Administration.

In the new organization, auditing of tax returns is divided into two major areas; field audit cases and office audit cases. The concept of office audit cases (cases involving small tax liability) was new to the Internal Tax Service.

A pilot project was set up at the National Office to determine what procedures would be necessary to implement office audit throughout the country. Based upon the experience of the pilot project in Santiago, an Office Audit Training Course was developed and presented in each of the 14 zones throughout Chile. This training course made use of training aids developed during the pilot project.

One of the needs of a well-organized Training Department is the availability of reference materials that may be used by instructors as well as students. The National Office Training Department established a Central Library. This library includes a comfortably furnished reading room as well as other rooms

for the display of books and for storage. A librarian
has been placed in charge of the library. The library
presently includes over 8,000 volumes, consisting of
about 6,000 books and 2,000 pamphlets.

An information bulletin was prepared and issued.
It contains general information concerning library
procedures and an index of all titles now available
in the library.

Three hundred newly appointed inspectors began
training on March 2, 1964. The inspector's training
program had been completely revised by then to provide for alternate periods of classroom and on-the-
job training. In general, the one-year training
program is divided as shown in Table 1.

To follow through with this program, it was
necessary to revise training materials previously
used in the inspector's course. Volumes 5 through 9
of the Manual were used as text books. The first
phase of the course is concerned with basic knowledge
that permits review of Office Audit cases. The advance course prepared the inspectors for Field Audit
cases. These cases (Training Nos. 6-7) were prepared
in the same style and format as other recently completed training courses.

To meet the needs of supervisory personnel in
all divisions, plans had been formulated, as indicated
earlier, to have all supervisors complete the basic
course in Fundamentals of Supervision. The basic
course, covering 40 hours of classroom participation,
was followed by a specialized course of 2 to 5 additional days in the area of specialization of each
supervisor. Specialized courses for supervisors in
the areas of Audit, Processing and Tax Fraud have
been developed. The first of these specialized
courses, (Training Guide No. 3) dealing with the duties and responsibilities of the Group Chief in the
Audit Division was prepared and presented to all
audit Group Chiefs.

A system of reporting work progress, requiring
the use of statistical forms and information was approved for implementation throughout the country. Initial reporting under this program began March 1, 1964.
To thoroughly familiarize all personnel with the required forms and procedures for reporting work production, seminars and training sessions were scheduled
both at the National Office and at field offices
throughout the country.

TABLE 1

The One-Year Training Program

Weeks	Place	Explanation
2	School	Orientation and general training on use of forms and public relations.
4	Field (in an operating office)	Taxpayers' assistance programs.
8	School	Basic training for inspectors. Preparation for Office Audit type cases.
21	Field	On-the-job training and in-office audit procedures and cases.
7	School	Advanced training in field office techniques and procedures.
8	Field	On-the-job training in field audit.
2	-	Evaluations and summaries.
52		

In the development of training materials, the
use of visual aids and equipment assumes a position
of major importance. If there is to be a break with
tradition, training classes need them to increase
student participation. The Training Department has
been able to secure, for use in training programs,
the following equipment: 8mm. sound motion picture
projectors; tape recorders; opaque and overhead
projectors; 35mm. slide projectors; flip charts;
flannel boards; portable lecterns; and motion picture
and slide title machines.

To meet training needs at all levels, the Training Department has in some cases found it necessary
to cooperate with personnel and provide voluntary
after-hour courses. These courses were planned and
presented in answer to either a request made by employees' groups or a known need which could not be
met during regular work hours because of teaching
schedules. The following courses are illustrations
of this voluntary after-hour training program:

1. A general accounting course was conducted
for inspectors who did not have an accountant's title.
This course consisted of 196 classroom hours of instruction. The time devoted to the course exceeded
the number of hours required by local commercial
schools specializing in accounting programs. The
course was presented by the Chief of the Program Section of the Training Department, who taught the same
course at the University of Chile.
2. Following the reorganization, many lawyers
in the Legal Division felt a need to know something
about accounting in order to perform the legal duties
assigned to them. An accounting course for lawyers
was organized to give elementary accounting principles. This course covered a period of 5 weeks and
consisted of daily sessions of one hour each.
3. Clerks of the service, in an attempt to
secure advancement, requested accounting training.
There was no provision in the personnel procedures
that permited credit for in-service training courses.
The Training Department, however, provided facilities
and space for use of the trainees, so that they could
complete accounting courses.

A course for special agents was prepared and
presented to all agents in the Tax Fraud Department.
The training course began March 9, 1964. Sessions
were held twice weekly for 1 1/2 hours each day. The
material prepared for the course was used as a basis

for a special agents' handbook. The course covered
both procedural knowledge as well as knowledge required in the planning and conducting of investigations.

The internal organization of the Training Department has kept pace with other programs conducted by
the Department. In November 1963, an Internal Manual
of Instructions for personnel of the Training Department was prepared and distributed to all employees of
the department. This manual contains descriptions
and responsibilities of all work assignments, as well
as a listing of delegation of authority. This manual
has been used as an example for other departments in
the development of job assignments.

The Chilean Tax Administration school has become
well known throughout South America and over the last
three years various countries have sent staff members
to attend specific courses. In 1966 the Chilean Tax
Service offered the use of the school to all South
America as a contribution to the Alliance for Progress. In February 1967 the first international class
met with participants from all over South America.
The first course was on Instructor Training and Administration of a Training School. Courses in Supervision, Tax Fraud, Auditing and Investigation are
scheduled for the future. It is hoped and expected
that the school will become a center of training in
Tax Administration for all Latin America.

(A list of the training courses available as of
1966 and an organization chart of the school is presented in Appendix D.)

CHAPTER **6** INTERNAL
COMMUNICATIONS

Through a program spanning four years and more
than 185,000 man-hours of work, the Chilean Tax
Service was provided with a modern, efficient manual
system of communication which permits instructions
and norms to be transmitted to offices throughout the
country with rapidity and accuracy. It has resulted
in a more uniform interpretation of laws and regulations and a more equal treatment of taxpayers, whether
in a rural village or Santiago.

Without a manual system of communications, it
would have been impossible to delegate authority to
the lowest office levels, since delegation of authority without proper communication of policy and program
becomes anarchy. In addition, the thousands of man-
hours saved through the ready availability of all instructions and interpretations of law was put to
better use in auditing taxpayers' returns.

REVIEW OF THE
COMMUNICATIONS SYSTEM

The development of a manual system of communications for the Internal Tax Service in Chile began
with a review of the communications system as it
prevailed in May 1961. After many visitations and
discussions with Service officials and employees,
both in the National Office and in Field Offices
throughout Chile, the Director of the Tax Service was
convinced that the methods of communicating instructions and policies to personnel of the Service were
inadequate. They were deficient in several respects:

1. Instructions were published by means of
numbered circulars issued by each of the several
national office departments with little relation of
one to another.

2.   Instructions were still in force which had been issued many years before, and it was becoming increasingly difficult to know with full certainty which were current and which were not.

3.   The information in the circulars neither dealt with a single subject nor was arranged by subject matter, and no index of any type was available for reference purposes. Thus it was most difficult to know whether one had all the information current on a particular subject.

4.   There was no filing system established for this information; the circulars could be found almost anywhere, principally in disarray in employees' desk drawers.

5.   Many instructions were unwritten; certain procedures and policies were followed simply because of long experience. This situation obviously made for considerable difficulty, even under the existing organization of the Service, wherein the decision-making was done largely at the national level and a pooling of knowledge and long experience was centrally available.
     With the introduction of a completely new organization based upon greater delegation of responsibility and decentralization, the need for a more adequate system of communications became even greater.

6.   The laws and regulations were not available to the staff of the Service except through purchase of the sections.

7.   No basic instructions for the training of new personnel was available.

The problem was presented to and discussed with the top personnel, and they, too, felt that an improved communications system was essential to successful implementation of the reorganization. During these discussions, the development of a loose-leaf manual which would readily be maintained in a current status was agreed to by the Director as meeting the needs of the Service.

The management values of a good communication system include the following:

1.   Communications channeling. The most obvious advantage to management is having clearly designated

and recognized channels of official communication.
The status of nonauthenticated publications is not
left to conjecture for management or employees.

    2. Organization control and planning. If em-
ployees are to work together harmoniously, clear-cut
divisions of labor must be made so that each will do
his assigned task and so that no necessary tasks will
be unassigned. If the separate work units, newly established, are to work toward the common goals harmoniously and effectively, definite relationships
must be established in the form of lines of communication, review, work flow, etc. Logically organized
manuals of functional statements, operating policies,
responsibilities, and procedures are, in a sense, a
graphic portrayal of the physiology of organization.
They provide a framework for review and analysis.
    Planning for the future must necessarily be
conducted in the light of past and present experience.
Written records document such experience for ready
reference. They prevent the making of continued
mistakes that were previously corrected.

    3. Standardization. Control of operations de-
pends upon standardization of routines and specification of the manner in which exceptions should be
handled. Operations which are standardized can be
controlled from afar and integrated with other activities. This is especially true in National Office
control of field operations. Specification of work
methods is a prerequisite to fixing work standards
and measuring performance. Manuals and standard
practice instructions are the vehicles for communicating these standardized methods.

    4. Audit and review. The operating manual is
of value in conducting performance audits. Examinations can be made of actual practices and perfor-
mances against prescribed methods and criteria.
Deviations and unworkable methods can be identified
for study and possible correction. Official written
instructions are relied upon by internal auditors as
the ruling criteria for audits of fiscal paper.

    5. Public relations. Every employee who comes
into contact with the public is a special public relations representative. He must know the answers
(or where to find them) to a great number of questions.
His manuals and circulars are indispensable for this
purpose. Moreover, increased mobility causes the
public to expect the same type of service from different branches of the Tax Service.

If the system is installed correctly, many other benefits also accrue. By "correctly" we mean participation in the development of the changes and preparation of the manual by all department heads, supervisors and as wide a scope of individuals as possible. This is a key factor in obtaining staff acceptance of change.

If installation and development of the manual is approached this way, we can expect:

1. Overlapping, duplication and conflict to be identified and eliminated.
2. Important gaps to be identified for developmental attention.
3. Defects in methods to be revealed and often improved during the course of compilation.
4. Unnecessary or obsolete activities to be eliminated.
5. The number of forms required to be reduced.
6. Responsibilities and authorities to be clarified.
7. Organizational relationships to be improved through the bringing of interdependent activities into common focus and examination.
8. The participation of employees in the examination of the why and how of operations to stimulate their work interest, improve their knowledge of operations, and develop their analytical abilities.

DEVELOPMENT OF THE PROJECT PLAN

Following the Director's general acceptance of an operating manual for the Service, a project plan was developed which outlined the organization and the procedures under which the manual would be prepared and the manner in which the project would be administered.

Basically, the plan established a Central Coordination and Control Unit to carry out the responsibilities inherent in its title and groups of writers, each administered by a coordinator, in each department of the Chilean Tax Service to prepare material for the Manual.

The Central Unit was initially composed of the advisor in organization and methods and two Chilean technicians from the Service's Department of Organization and Methods. Ultimately the responsibility

for administering the manual system was to be assigned
to this department; accordingly, the assignment of
members of its staff to the project had a practical
and long-term purpose.

The draft material flowed from the writers
through the Group Coordinator to the Central Unit of
the Steering Committee for initial review and for
conformity with established guidelines, back to the
groups for revision and submission to Department
Chiefs for final approval, thence to the Central Unit
for final conversion to manual style and preparation
of Multilith masters, and finally to the appropriate
department of the Service for reproduction, assembly,
and distribution. As the process developed, the
Central Unit also assumed responsibility for reproduction and assembly prior to distribution.

By June 1962, the development of a manual system
had been discussed informally and in general terms
only by a few of the top personnel. The first step
then was to brief all the key personnel (i.e., Department Chiefs) in the proposed system and the
project plan and explain their responsibilities in
connection with the preparation of the manual. This
was done in a conference held on June 19, 1962, during
which each Department Chief was asked to designate two
or three technicians on his staff to work full-time
on the manual.

Before the job was completed the work had been
shared by almost the entire National Office, as is
shown in Table 2. There were at times as many as 150
personnel, both National Office and field staff,
working on the manual.

A specific effort was made to obtain participation of field personnel in the preparation of the
manual to ensure consideration of field problems and
experience.

It must be understood that the basic system of
a manual for the Service and the determination that
nine separate volumes were required were the subject
of considerable debates and discussions prior to the
launching of the project. These discussions were
held by the advisor with the Chilean technicians of
the Department of Organization and Methods and many
of the key officials and other technicians of the
Service. Only after these discussions were the final
guidelines which best met the needs of the Service
drawn.

TABLE 2

Preparation of the Tax Service Manual

Vol.	Title	Responsible Offices
I	Organization and General Administration	Department of Organization and Methods, Personnel, Budget and Accounting, Information and Diffusion
II	Internal Procedures (Processing)	Department of Planning Department of Machines
III	Auditing	Audit Standards Department
IV	Tax Fraud	Tax Fraud Department
V	General Policies on Taxes	Legal Department
VI	Income Tax	Income Tax Department
VII	Sales Tax	Sales Tax Department
	Service Tax	Income Tax Department
VIII	Property Tax	Property Tax Department
	Inheritance Tax	Legal Department
IX	Alcohol Tax	Alcohol Department
X	Stamp & Misc. Taxes	Acts & Contracts Department

Four volumes were to be of an internal nature
concerning matters of administration and procedure
within the Service; the other five volumes were to
be the "Prentice-Hall" or "Commerce Clearing House"
of Chilean tax law and regulation. It was projected
that they be used not only by the Service personnel,
but subsequently be made available for sale to tax
practitioners.

INTERNAL COMMUNICATIONS
REQUIREMENTS

This preliminary planning is of the greatest
importance. The inherent instruction requirements
for any tax agency are similar. In addition to the
situational similarities, there are variances caused
by differences in operating environment, and their
requirements. There are two major factors which require consideration.

Organization Factors

1. Age and maturity. The established organization installing a system for the first time has a
problem of mass inventory and codification. Its
major problem of installation is to overcome resis-
tances. For a substantial period, a great deal of
attention would have to be given to simplification,
elimination of overlapping and conflicts, and correction of obsolescence. Gaps need to be filled.
Thereafter, the rate of release should settle down to
a norm for that organization. The "who-needs-what"
should be reasonably simple to ascertain.
A young organization goes through much trial
and error. It needs great flexibility in releasing
and revising instructions. If part or all of an old
organization undergoes a major work change, it assumes characteristics of a new organization for purposes of designing an instructions system.

2. Form of organization. The important organizational factors include the degree to which operations are under centralized or decentralized control
and the extent to which the activities of separate
units are integrated. In a sense, both are related.
There tends to be a higher degree of central control
when departments or divisions are interdependent.
This suggests an overall system of instructional coordination.
When operating discretion is decentralized
(as it should be in a tax service) the central

emphasis is on establishment of standards and systems
and post-audit review of the action of the subsidiary
departments or divisions. In a decentralized operation, central instructions are usually confined to
basic policy, programs, systems, and standards.
Accounting and reporting procedures also are usually
released centrally.

     3. Size. The element of size runs through most
of the other points to be discussed. Instructional
situations are often created by sheer size. This is
true of interpretation of regulations and law management and common administrative services.

     Size brings forth specialization and com-
plexity. Employees in a big organization tend to lose
sight of the whole in their preoccupation with their
own work. The need for indoctrination material for
uniformity of taxpayer treatment is increased--perhaps
geometrically--in a large organization. In many instances only through reference to written materials
is it possible to find out about work policies and
practices in another part of the organization. In a
large organization, the rule dominates; exceptions or
latitude for individual deviation are discouraged in
order to preserve discipline. The larger the number
of people or units performing similar operations, the
greater is the necessity for written standardization.
Any tax service over 1,500 people can be considered
large in this definition.

     4. Growth or expansion. An expansion trend will
create a demand for instructional materials, particularly if the trend is toward opening more field offices. Ready availability of manuals is a great asset
in putting a new office on an operational basis as
quickly as possible. It eliminates the confusion and
delay which occur while the Field Office attempts to
get instructions from the National Office on the
treatment of problems as they arise.

     5. Geography and space relationships. If half
a dozen people working in one room require instructions applicable to them only, the instructions can
be oral or by simple memorandum. If these people are
dispersed in the same building, throughout the city,
or in the field, a need is created for progressively
more formal, written instructions. Thus, the crux
of any headquarters-field relationship is the adequacy
and effectiveness of the communication system.

6. Availability of guidelines. In standard operations, for which there are adequate guidelines, many things need not be spelled out. When operations are of a unique or unprecedented nature, they require more detailed instructional guidance. With new legislation continually being passed on taxation, the instructional system for a tax agency needs to be flexible, expandable, and readily adaptable.

7. Need for uniformity. Certain operations must be performed identically to enable a National Office to perform its central operations. This is especially true where accounting and statistical information must be collated or utilized. There is also a public relations aspect, because people who live in different locations expect uniform treatment from different offices of the tax service.

8. Complexity and precision. The need for precise, carefully coordinated instructions becomes greater with any increase in the complexity or intricate character of an organization and its methods. In a tax service the parts of the operation must be carefully timed and must fit together accurately. Complete and precise instructions must be passed on to the units and individuals involved. Each link in the chain of operation must know what is expected of it and how it ties into the preceding and succeeding links.

9. Degree of internal change. In general, all Tax Services which have a great deal of internal activity and change, including changes in law, regulation, method, and staff, need a system which is flexible and readily adaptable to revision. The distribution system must permit those who actually need operating instructions to receive them with a minimum of delay. On the other hand, an organization which is fairly well settled and has little change in internal activity, has less need for extensive flexibility and revisibility in its media of instructional release. A tax service with its constantly changing laws falls into the first category.

Personnel Factors

1. Turnover. Excessive personnel turnover places a greater demand upon production of instruction materials for use in training and indoctrination. Wider distribution of instructions is necessary.

2. Caliber. The caliber of personnel will govern the format and style of instructions as well as the degree of detail and specificity. The governing factors are the intelligence, training, and experience of the personnel. Instructions for a clerical group require a different written and visual treatment than for a group of higher grade personnel. Sometimes, instructions on the same subject must be prepared in a separate series with different style treatment, if there is too great a difference in levels of comprehension. The necessity for clearly written instructions is made greater as less reliance can be placed on the judgment capacity of employees.

On June 25, 1962, all Group Coordinators in the Communications Manual Project were briefed on the project and their responsibilities; on July 5, the training session for writers and coordinators was held; then the real work commenced.

PROGRESS OF THE PLAN

The first step in the process, that of preparing a tentative table of contents for the material, was considered of prime importance to the quality of the end product. However, thinking in terms of specific parts of a broad subject and attempting to prepare a fairly comprehensive "outline" before beginning to write was a concept of considerable difficulty to impart. After several weeks of laborious work and draft upon draft of revised tables of contents, a tentative outline acceptable to the Central Unit was prepared for each of the nine volumes and the groups proceeded to the next steps, i.e. the review of existing instructions, the screening out of obsolete and duplicate instructions, the recognition of areas wherein written instructions were nonexistent and, finally, based upon the results of the preceding steps, the preparation of the manual instructions in draft form.

Regular meetings were held once each week attended by all the coordinators and the members of the Central Unit. During these meetings, each coordinator reported on progress during the previous week and raised any question or problem which his group had encountered on which there was doubt about the best approach to take. At the same time the Central Unit reported on any developments affecting the project as a whole and announced any new guidelines or decisions that had been taken.

In this way, it was possible to obtain greater coordination among the groups and resolve problems or establish criteria which would best serve the interests of the greater number. From time to time, written instructions or guidelines were issued to the work groups on matters which were of particular importance.

As the work groups proceeded to prepare material for the manual, the Central Unit concentrated on (1) the development of details of the manual system and (2) planning and arranging for the material needs of the project and the actual production of the material. It was necessary to reach a decision on many aspects of the system including:

1. Responsible authorities, including those authorized to sign instructions published under the system.
2. Procedures to be followed within the National Office in order to publish manual instructions.
3. The specific media by which manual changes, supplemental instructions, and information would be published.
4. The distribution system and distribution formulas.

All of these points were the subject of careful study by the Central Unit and were discussed with those officials concerned in order to reach general accord. In some instances, approval by the "top steering committee," designated by the Director and referred to previously under "Organization," was required. The entire system was ultimately included in the Manual as Chapter 8, Volume I. (See Appendix B).

Until December 1962, the prime motivation for the manual was the simple need for improved administrative communications which in theory could begin to function whenever the manual was ready. However, with the approval in December 1962, of the Organic Act restructuring the Tax Service, another element entered the picture. The provisions of the act were to be implemented on July 1, 1963. It then became essential to complete, at a minimum, the first four volumes dealing with internal administration and operating procedures to use for staff training before that date. Reorganization had no direct bearing on the last five volumes dealing with tax doctrine, and thus they were not subject to this new pressure.

During the entire preceding period, personnel
had been working continuously on Volume II, Internal
Procedures; Volume III, Auditing; and Volume IV, Tax
Fraud; and this new factor required acceleration of
the work and, in some instances, additional personnel.

The chapters of Volume I, Administration, dealing with organization, functions, and delegation of
authority were handled in a slightly different way.
Special task forces were formed by personnel drawn
from both the National and Field Offices and organized on a functional basis, i.e. top management,
administrative services, legal, planning and studies,
processing (tax operations) and auditing. Their
mission was to develop in detail the organization,
functions, and delegation of authority for their
respective areas at all levels throughout the Service.
A "top steering committee," consisting of the proposed Subdirectors and Regional Directors and the
advisor, which was established to guide the reorganization of the Service was also made responsible for
reviewing all material prepared by these task forces.
Following this review and subsequent approval by the
Director, the material was revised to the extent
necessary for incorporation in the manual by the
Department of Organization and Methods.

In March 1963, in view of the pressure to complete the first four volumes and the tremendous
quantity of typing work to be done on other volumes,
a typing pool of sixteen people was formed under the
direction of the Central Unit. This pool of personnel
was to type draft material for the work groups and
special task forces and prepare the Multilith mats
of approved material for reproduction in manual form.
As the work subsequently evolved, this typing pool,
assisted to some extent by the personnel in the
Service's Printing and Binding Unit, which also
operated under the direction of the Central Control
Unit, provided the assembly work necessary on the
Manual.

This entire group of typing and reproduction
personnel worked overtime continuously from March to
June; the overtime then continued until December 1963,
in an effort to produce the remaining volumes as soon
as possible. At this point, even though all volumes
had not been completed, it was decided that the personnel had absorbed all the extra work they could and
the overtime was terminated.

The first four volumes were produced and made available in sufficient quantity for the massive training program undertaken on July 1, 1963. During the following six weeks, all personnel in the Service were oriented, during a training period ranging from 2 to 5 days, in the new organization, concepts, procedures and delegations, using the manual volumes as a basis for instruction. Also during the six-week period these four volumes were made ready for general distribution, and they were finally distributed throughout the Service on August 16, 1963.

In the meanwhile, the original work groups, changed somewhat in composition because of transfers of personnel due to pressure of other work and the demands of reorganization, continued their work on the other five volumes. These volumes were printed and distributed throughout the Service as they became available as indicated below:

Volume VII	Service Tax	Oct. 17, 1963
Volume VIII	Property Tax	Nov. 26, 1963
Volume VII	Sales Tax	Dec. 11, 1963
Volume V	General Tax Policies	Feb. 3, 1964
Volume IX	Stamp and Misc. Taxes	March 1, 1964
Volume IX	Alcohol Tax	April 1964
Volume VI	Income Tax	April 10, 1964
Volume VIII	Inheritance Tax	July 16, 1964

With the publication of the Inheritance Tax section of Volume VIII, the major work of creating a Manual was complete.

Some concept of the immensity of this task and the tremendous accomplishment it represents can be realized when one considers the following:

   a) A set of the volumes printed thus far contains approximately 2,100 sheets of paper and 4,000 single spaced printed pages.
   b) The volumes were printed in quantities ranging from 200 to 1,200 copies each.
   c) They represent approximately 3,750,000 printing impressions.
   d) A minimum of 2,000,000 sheets of paper were used in the process of printing.
   e) A fully accurate estimate of the man-hours dedicated to the project is impossible to obtain. However, a recapitulation of the personnel assigned specifically to this work indicated that through July 1964, considerably

more than 185,000 man-hours had been invested
in its completion. This figure does not include unknown factors such as uncompensated
overtime and the time of Department Chiefs
and many other personnel who were involved
either directly or indirectly in the investigative, conciliation, and review phases
of the project.

The manual communication system, in terms of
achieving the goal of the Tax Service, is a basic requirement and is well worth the cost and trouble.

1. Equal and uniform treatment of all taxpayers
under law and regulation.
2. Complete, accurate and uniform information
to the public at all offices.
3. Delegation of authority which permits quick
and accurate handling of taxpayers in each geographical location. Without a method that delineates programs and systems in detail, delegation of authority
is operationally unworkable.
4. Confidence on the part of all staff in their
ability to handle taxpayers, since the information
they need is readily available.
5. Increase of staff time on action and decrease
of time spent on research.
6. A base for training of staff.
7. A base for change and improvement and a
method for communicating it.
8. A method for coordination of different functions.

CHAPTER **7** AUDIT: APPROACH
AND TECHNIQUES

The audit function, as noted previously, is one
of the two basic functions of any tax system. The
auditing of the taxpayer's books is the usual means
whereby respect for the tax service in finding and
punishing evasion is developed. On the effectiveness
of this function hinges the percentage of tax evasion
that each country will have.

It is impossible to have enough agents to audit
all tax returns. Generally the number of returns to
be audited should range from 2 to 3 per cent of the
returns filed in the countries with the lease amount
of evasion up to 7 to 8 per cent in those countries
with the greatest amount of evasion. Unfortunately
those countries who need an 8 per cent audit coverage
are usually those which lack the audit staff.

Generally, given a proportionate number of agents,
there is a tendency toward the audit assessments being higher in comparison to the total amount of tax
intake in those countries where the evasion is greatest. The proportion of audit assessments to total
tax paid in recent years, as an example, has been
slightly less than 2 per cent in the United States,
about 4 1/2 per cent in Chile, and approximately 5 to
6 per cent in Argentina.

If we can generally agree, therefore, that the
assessments made by audit are a very small percentage
of any tax intake, the purposes of the function must
be not to secure money or assessments but to secure
the general compliance of the tax-paying public. This
shifts the entire planning and programming of the
function and makes it more of an art than an exact
accounting science.

Audit operations, therefore, should be programmed
to get the maximum coverage of taxpayers with the
staff that is available. The percentage of coverage

68

would vary with the percentage of evasion. A country
where the evasion rate on income or sales tax is 50
per cent or more would need a 6 per cent to 8 per
cent audit coverage of audit returns to start its
program. As the rate of evasion decreases, the percentage of coverage can decrease with it.

A BALANCED AUDIT PROGRAM

Following the above points as a base, therefore,
the development of a balanced audit program envisages
that each audit should be chosen to have the greatest
possible impact on the taxpaying public.

Tax returns should be carefully selected so that
the utmost would be secured from the ripple effect.
(As with a stone thrown into a pond, the coverage is
greater when the second stone is placed where the
ripples of the first one reach their furthest limit.)
One would not audit small commercial stores right
next to each other or more than a carefully selected
sample of business firms in each industry. If an
aura of the infallibility of the tax service is to be
developed, all segments of the taxpaying public must
feel that they are likely to be audited.

This is accomplished by auditing a percentage of
all groups from the largest to the smallest--indus-
tries, professionals, tradesmen--all carefully selected by size and geography to have the widest effect.
Each audit should pay for itself many times over by
other taxpayers expecting an audit because of the
comments of those who have been audited. This in turn
makes for valid voluntary payment in anticipation of
the possible audit.

There is nothing quite as useless in the long run
as the raids on specific industries where everyone is
given a quick audit and in which everyone knows,
since other industries will receive the same treatment,
they themselves will not be audited again for a period
of years.

To accomplish the above goal, audit is usually
divided into three functional areas: field audit,
office and mail audit and taxpayer assistance.

1. Field Audit - Field audit, as indicated by
its name, usually consists of qualified accountants
who audit those businesses which, because of their

size or complexity, require a complete tax audit.
This has to be done where the books and records are
available and where inventory and other items can be
checked on the spot. These audits usually consume a
considerable amount of time, and, because of seasonal
factors in various businesses, have to be scheduled
carefully. A yearly program based on economic factors
and availability of staff is covered under Audit Capacity below.

2. Office and Mail Audit - Office audits are
quick audits on those taxpayers who are small enough,
i.e. professionals, small businesses, salary earners,
so that the books and records can be brought into the
office. The emphasis here is on quantity rather than
quality, since the cases are small and to achieve an
impact the greatest number possible of taxpayers must
be covered. Generally speaking, these audits should
not take more than half a day to a day and a half as
a maximum and the items audited should be pre-selected
and kept to a minimum. In this way the "presence" of
the tax service will be diffused over the whole
country.

When there is difficulty in contacting the
taxpayers because of distance and the items to be
checked are few and can be resolved with specific information, the audit can be done by mail. The results are generally not too satisfactory except for
omitted information and should normally be kept to a
minimum.

3. Taxpayer Assistance - This is the other face
of the tax service, the smiling face. In order to
emphasize this attitude, the tax service should make
every attempt to cooperate with those taxpayers who
need assistance. Special arrangements must be made
to give emphasis to helping the taxpayer in complying
with the law. For example, tax forms should be available at all times and telephone consultation groups
should be set up, especially during the filing period,
in order to answer questions that can be handled in
this manner. Groups of auditors should be retained
in the office, as necessary, to assist taxpayers who
come in with technical questions. The difficult part
of taxpayer assistance is to draw a fine line between
reasonable taxpayer assistance and making out the taxpayer's return for him, which is not necessarily considered the function of the tax service. As the
situation warrants, however, smaller taxpayers could
be given this service.

Audit Capacity

The first step in the preparation of an annual program is to determine the audit capacity--the number of returns that can be examined with the available audit staff.

The available audit staff is usually composed of office auditors and field agents. The office auditors may be grouped as those who will handle audits through correspondence and those who will conduct personal interviews.

The number of available field agents and office auditors is known at the time that the plan is being prepared (this is usually 6 months before the begin-ning of the year) and can be adjusted downward for the expected attrition through resignations, retire-ments, etc. and expanded for the additional personnel to be hired.

The number of available personnel in each group-ing is then converted into man-days (or hours) of work time to be provided. This is the total time (365 days) less nonwork days (Saturdays, Sundays, holidays, and an average of vacation time, sick leave and other leave). The remaining time is available work time. However, not all of this time can be applied to examination of taxpayer returns, since per-sonnel is needed for taxpayer assistance, selecting returns, reviewing completed work, training, etc. The proportion of this time to the total will depend on previous training of agents, the selection system and the need for review control. After this nonex-amination time has been deducted, the balance is available for audit programming.

The next step is to determine the total number of returns available for audit. This can be done using the returns filed if there is reasonable cer-tainty that most taxpayers who are required to file actually filed returns. This would presuppose an efficient Collection Division that picks up all de-linquent returns. If this is not the case economic studies should be the base.

The initial sorting of the returns usually is by size for business entities and wage earners and by geographical location for the professionals.

The next decision is the amount (percentage) of coverage to be provided to each group. In making this decision it should be noted that large businesses, with staffs of tax accountants and lawyers, often try to avoid taxation by finding loopholes in the law, covering inventory methods, special deductions and allocation of charges. Small businesses and professionals tend toward outright evasion by nonreporting of sales and services. Medium size businesses can go either way depending on the situation. A study of the above situation as it applies in any one country is the key consideration on which type of agent to assign to aduit the books of a taxpayer.

When the total amount of direct examination time is allocated to the various groups of returns, a computation is made converting this time into taxpayers to be examined. This is the first point at which the need for separate groupings of returns is demonstrated, because the time required to complete an examination varies with type of tax and size of return. Estimates of the time needed to complete an examination are based on many factors, such as whether it will be a field or office audit, the number of years to be examined, and the complexity of the examination. However, these estimates can be reasonably accurate based on time standards developed after one to two years of operation plus an analysis of the auditing requirements of each case and its relationship to the standard.

The length of time for auditing various types of cases usually will not be accurate for any one case. If complete records are maintained, however, the average time for each computed on a yearly basis can be estimated very closely.

The number of taxpayers to be audited is determined by dividing the man-days allocated to each segment by the man-days required to audit each taxpayer.

The next step is to determine the source of the examinations or number to be selected for examinations. The first consideration is the number of taxpayers that will be in the process of examination at the end of the current year plus the number of taxpayers assigned for examination. (This is assuming a continuing audit operation.) If this beginning inventory is excessive at the end of the current year a decision must be made whether the cases assigned will be disposed of without examination or whether they will be

examined. If they are to be examined, the number of
taxpayers to be selected will be reduced by this decrease in inventory anticipated.

Consideration will also have to be given to examinations that may be generated because of informant
letters, claims, bank reports or other reasons. These
sources will usually provide a substantial number of
examinations for consideration.

We have now come to the point where the final
selection of the number of returns to be audited will
be made. The two major factors of consideration are
the coverage to ensure compliance (by causing every
firm to believe there is a good possibility of being
audited every year) and, secondarily within that
framework, the securing of the greatest return of
money (both in terms of specific assessments by the
Internal Revenue agent and by the auditing of those
segments of the economy where voluntary compliance
would give the greatest money return).

Audit Selection

One of the general tools used here involves audit
standards by industry which give the key factors and
cross checks to be made in evaluating a tax return
and the tolerances permitted in the various interrelationships. This permits the selection of those
returns most likely to be fallacious within each industry group. The second method is the economic
studies of the nation which indicate the industries
that during the year or during a given time period
have had the greatest profit increase and those who
have had a bad year. It is at both extremes that the
tendency for tax avoidance or evasion becomes the
greatest. Third, a detailed map of the area is needed
to ensure geographic coverage, especially for small
businesses, wage earners and professionals. A very
important help in this type of decision is the availability of careful economic studies that show the
evasion percentage by industry, by various sizes of
firms, by geographic areas, etc. This will permit
pinpointing of the entire planning process.

Great care must be exercised to vary the above
factors. As the accountants and lawyers in the profession learn the criteria used for audit selection
they will use that knowledge in the preparation of
their clients' returns. The interrelationships between tax practitioners and the tax service

should always be close and, hopefully, courteous.
Knowledge of the selection criteria used to decide
which firms are to be audited each year, however,
would destroy the entire concept of audit so important
for voluntary compliance. Rigid selection criteria,
especially of the type used for primary selection by
data processing machines, are very subject to this
danger.

There are several other factors to be considered
in programming an audit function for a year.

Usually the process is started some six months
before the end of the year in order that the economic
studies can be made and the Field Offices who actually
do the field audit can be consulted. The guidelines
for the yearly audit program are usually developed
by audit and planning specialists in the National Office and should reach the operating offices some three
months before the beginning of the audit program
period.

The actual organization of the audit function
will determine to a great extent how the program will
be carried out. If the agents are specialized by industry groups, the auditing is not only faster but
much better as the information needed to do a good
audit, the approach to it, and the location of information are all well known. Specialist groups, in
addition, can provide the necessary geographical distribution and can be controlled to ensure that the
work actually and specifically is performed, as
selected.

In order that the agents do not become too specialized, a rotation system of agents (every three to
five years) will ensure a reasonably broad knowledge
of all industries while maintaining the specialized
knowledge of the group. This system usually requires
a bit more money for travel and possible discontent
of the agents being away from home. With careful
planning, however, this can be kept to a minimum.

With the program developed, the selection of
cases decided and standards of accomplishment set, it
is now up to each operating office to carry out the
program and achieve the agreed-on goals. The statistics of the performance of each audit unit in achieving these goals is the main audit control exercised
by the executive function.

An important consideration in carrying out the program is the approach to field audit (the tax audit). A tax audit is completely different than the usual accounting audit. Recognition of this fact and the training of agents in how to make a tax audit is basic to both quality and quantity performance. Standards as to the time necessary for an average audit by industry and size of firm must be based on "tax audits," not accounting audits.

FIELD AUDIT PROCEDURES

There are several types of audits made by public accounting firms, the most common being the year-end audit to determine the financial position of the company. It is essentially a balance sheet audit; in other words, an audit of each asset and liability of a company to determine that the assets are worth at least as much as the amount shown and that the liabilities are no more than the amount shown. The accountant is interested primarily in conservatism and consistency; in other words, that asset values are not overstated (they can be substantially understated in the name of conservatism) and that the method used to value assets is consistent with that used in prior years. The word consistent should not be confused with accurate. For example, an inventory may be valued at several million dollars below current market cost and value, but if a method consistent with that of prior years is used, such as standard cost (an artificial figure used as cost based on ideal purchase prices plus ideal costs of production and ideal overhead expenses), the accountant feels justified in certifying to the correctness of the balance sheet since the values are not overstated and are consistent. In other words, he could not be held liable if the taxpayer secured a loan on the basis of his certified balance sheet (the most common purpose for these certified statements) since the creditor could not say that the loan was not properly secured. The accountant is not too interested in the profit and loss statement except to insure that income and expenses related to balance sheet items are properly accrued at the end of each year. This again is done in the name of consistency, since they are certifying that they have satisfied themselves that the company is following a consistent policy regarding their accounts. They do not usually get involved in the question of income or deductions but accept company policy for these.

Therefore, unless specifically requested by their client to make a value audit (when a sale of assets or merger of a corporation is contemplated) or a security audit (when theft or embezzlement are suspected), the accountant does not make an income tax audit, that is, an audit to determine that the correct income is reported as defined by the Internal Revenue Code. In fact there are many recognized and accepted accounting practices that are directly opposed to the provisions of the Code.

An income tax audit, for example, can therefore be defined as one that has as its objective the determination of the substantially correct income. (This statement can be modified to cover "value" in estate and gift tax cases and cost of "manufacturing" or "sales" in the case of sales or excise taxes.) The computation of the correct tax on the determination is provided in the Tax Code.

This type of audit is directed to those items that, if incorrect, may materially change the profit or loss of a business. The examiner then uses a system of testing, sampling, and scanning to determine the problem areas and the depth of auditing needed to resolve the questions.

The word audit is probably a misnomer, since the practice is more an investigation of a business activity. It can probably be explained best by taking specific types of cases and following the audit and/or investigative steps involved.

Auditing Small Businesses or Professionals

Small businesses are usually operated on a cash basis, that is, cash and checks are received for sales and services and most expenses are paid daily with cash. The owner of the business handles the money and most of the record keeping. Therefore, there is very little internal control for cash or other transactions such as pre-numbered receipts or invoices. The business is really run out of the man's pocket, cash box, or cash register. These factors must be considered when planning the audit and the agent must familiarize himself with the peculiarities of this type of business or profession. This is a part of the first audit step called "pre-examination planning."

Pre-examination planning is thinking of what is to be done and how to do it. The general approach which is valid for all sizes and types of audit includes:

a. Familiarizing oneself with the business.
b. Examining the tax return to determine which items will be checked and the possible problems to be encountered.
c. Preparing a list of points to be covered in the initial interview with the taxpayer.

The second step is the informal discussion with the taxpayer when he is first contacted. This is a most important period since it usually is the last time that the taxpayer will be "open" in his discussions. The discussion sets the tone of the audit. Carefully handled, it will be friendly and lead to cooperation. Improperly handled, it will result in friction and delays in securing information. The discussion must be conversational and not a questioning session. The taxpayer should do the talking about his hobbies, interests, vacations, family, and finally his business, outside business interests and his banking habits. It is important that he explain how and by whom cash receipts and disbursements are controlled. Finally, agreement should be reached on who will answer questions and provide information required during the audit. A tour of the business premises should be made at this time.

After the discussion, the examiner should prepare a brief summary of his discussion, noting pertinent information regarding the taxpayer's financial situation such as cost of hobbies, interests and vacations, children's education, home, furnishing, car, clothing, etc. The ideal arrangement would be to conduct the interview in the taxpayer's home, but since it is usually done at the place of business, the examiner should drive past the taxpayer's home either the day before or the day the audit begins. He should also note the controls or lack of controls discussed and other peculiarities of the business.

Next, the agent should use at least two alternative methods for determining whether gross sales or profit are substantially correct. This is the most important, and frequently the only, item to be verified on a small business return, since deductions are usually nominal. These alternative methods for a retail grocery may be, for example:

1.   Prepare a typical shopping list for a week's
groceries (meat, butter, eggs, flour, etc.).   Take
this list and note the prices shown on these items in
the store.   Check the purchase invoice price for these
items.   Compute the gross profit and compare it to the
gross profit reported and percentage mark-up.   This
method is effective if purchases are substantially
correct.

2.   Total all deposits to the business and personal bank accounts and savings accounts.   Add all
cash expenditures for business and personal items
(the taxpayer's personal items can be determined by
using a questionnaire for covering all items and securing answers to how much was spent for each of them
in the current week or month rather than one or two
years ago).   This total is compared to gross sales.

In the case of a doctor an examiner can:

1.   Determine the office hours maintained during
a week from his appointment book.   Approximate the
number of home calls made.   Compute the fees received
from these sources based on the charge per half-hour
visit.   Add any known special charges and compare to
total receipts.

2.   Check with hospitals where the doctor practices to determine number of operations, deliveries,
etc. and check against patient cards.

3.   Check record of payments by insurance companies such as Blue Cross or Medicare and compare to
records.

4.   Check gross receipts as explained in (2)
above.

These preliminary audit steps should not take
more than one to two days if properly planned and
skillfully executed.

When substantial differences are noted in sales,
gross income, net profit or other specific items, the
scope and depth of the audit is increased to determine
whether a pattern of evasion exists.   Man, being a
creature of habit, usually establishes some systematic
method of concealment.   Even in the most ingenious
evasion schemes there is a pattern.   Usually those
who are greedy and conceited will feel that if a
method has been used without detection for a period
of time, it can be accelerated in amount and frequency.
Therefore, the examiner must look for the pattern such
as not recording sales of a certain type, decreasing
sales by a consistent amount each day, week or month,

charging personal expenses to certain accounts, depositing money in specifiè banks (usually a bank in a city near a usual vacation spot or a frequently visited relative). The auditor must ask himself, "If I were in this type of business, operating under these conditions, how would I evade tax?"

Very often, discussions with employees will disclose the pattern followed, since they may knowingly or unknowingly be involved. When a pattern is established, it is usually a simple process to follow it into prior and/or subsequent years.

If it is not possible to get the same information for prior years because older records are no longer available (or concealed), the usual method for determining a taxpayer's income over a period of years is used--the "net worth" method.

The net worth method is a reconstruction of a person's value at two or more specific periods of time--usually the beginning of the first year open by the statute of limitations and the end of the last year for which a tax return was due. This reconstruction involves the preparation of a statement of all of the assets and liabilities and a statement of personal expenses. It may be obtained simply by questioning a cooperative taxpayer and using his books and records. It may also be obtained from banks or other financial institutions where a financial statement has been submitted in order to secure a loan. The beginning net worth (assets less liabilities) is compared to the ending net worth in order to determine the amount of increase. The estimated living expense for the years between are added to the increase to determine how much income was earned during this period. This income is compared to the income reported on the tax returns to determine the income not reported.

Auditing Medium-Size Businesses

A medium-size business is usually operated as a partnership or corporation. In both of these types of operation it is necessary to examine not only the business records but also the personal records of the partners or corporate officers at the same time. In other words, in order to reconstruct gross or net income from the business, it is necessary to reconstruct the correct income of the individual partners or stockholders who may have diverted the funds from the business.

The medium-sized business combines the problems previously noted for small businesses with the more technical and sophisticated problems found in books and records of a larger company. This is especially true in family and closely held partnerships and corporations (partnerships, interests, or stock held by a few people).

In these businesses it is very important that internal controls be discussed during the initial interview. If the partners or officers do not have direct access to cash receipts but have employees handling cash, they usually have a good method of control over these employees. The examiner, therefore, must find the most likely point for withdrawal of funds in the system, after the cash has been handled by the employees.

If cash sales are deposited in the bank intact by a responsible employee, then the examiner must only be concerned with the transactions which are handled personally by the partners or officers. This is usually a special client, a special account or a type of transaction such as the sale of excess or scrap material, sales of assets, purchase or sales rebates, etc.

In those companies where the partners or officers have easy access to cash receipts and disbursements, the audit steps outlined for small business are followed to determine gross sales or gross profit. Then some additional time is spent scanning the largest accounts or unusual transactions shown in the books and records. The auditor must also analyze all entries to the partner's or officer's personal accounts.

As previously explained in the section dealing with small businesses, the examiner is constantly alert to patterns of evasion and schemes that have been found in similar types of business. Each taxpayer has this "key" which, when discovered, opens the door and discloses the method used to evade tax, if the evasion exists.

The audit steps taken in technical issues will follow in the discussion of large companies

Auditing Large Businesses

Large businesses usually have good accounting records and usually a system of internal control that

does not allow one person access to cash or other
assets. These companies also have internal and external auditors to prevent employees from embezzling
or otherwise cheating the company.

An agent can considerably shorten the time spent
auditing these companies if he understands the accounting system and the organizational structure including its reporting system. He uses these to
provide the information he needs. Much of this is
learned during the initial interview which differs
from that described for small and medium businesses
in that the discussion is centered on the type of
business, how it operates, the type of accounting
system, controls, and persons to be contacted for
various types of information. Agreement must be
reached on working space, help to be provided, and
available equipment.

The agent has already studied the tax return and
prior examination reports, if any, to determine which
large or unusual items must be examined. Now he must
study the chart of accounts, operating manual, internal and external audit reports, audit reports of other
regulatory agencies, stockholder reports, minute books
and data processing system manual, if used. These
will identify problem areas and the best method to
secure the needed information. The depth or scope of
the audit is based on the reliability of the accounting system and internal controls. For example, if
the operating manual provides that all expenses up
to $10,000 and all purchases up to $50,000 are handled
normally by personnel of the purchasing department,
accounting department, and disbursing department, and
the company and outside auditors periodically check
these items, the agent can merely review their reports
(internal audit and public accounting). His auditing
will be limited to items above these amounts handled
personally, by officers and stockholders.

He should also review all book entries and/or
adjustments in the books or between book and tax return figures since these are made by officers and
stockholders. Another example is the inventory problem. If outside accountants are employed for a year-
end audit, there is included a verification of the
yearend inventory, including personnel supervising
the taking of the inventory and its pricing. Therefore, the agent can audit the accountant's written
procedures for taking the inventory and the workpapers
showing the items checked by the accountants.

In companies lacking a good accounting and internal control system the scope of the audit is increased to include some of the audit checks usually made by public and internal auditors. However, these are limited to the large and unusual items and accounts until problems are found.

When problems are encountered in any audit, the agent is again to be aware of patterns or the "key" to what is being done and how it is done. The next most important consideration is <u>what</u> is needed to resolve the problem--this "what" is the difference between spending days, weeks or even months when a few hours may suffice. For example, an agent can find a substantial number of invoices for what appears to be funds spent building a $150,000 home for an officer. He can spend weeks going through all the invoices looking for this total sum when it could be done in one hour by asking for the contract to build the house (from either the company or contractor). Therefore, it is important to decide whether to ask to see an invoice, cancelled check, contract, lease, bill of sale, etc., (the document that will answer the question) rather than spend hours or days discussing and arguing about issues.

The tax return of the officers who have access to company funds (write checks, approve expenditures, etc.) should be examined concurrently because in all large corporations these officers receive substantial fringe benefits which may not be reported as income. Many of these are cloaked under legal provisions of the Code--granting them tax-exempt status; however, very frequently it is found that although they may appear to conform to the requirements of the Code and regulations, they do not when the contracts and agreements are examined closely. These include stock options, insurance policies, travel expenses, etc.

As is obvious from the above discussion, well-trained agents, specialized in areas of knowledge and kept current by an information system that keeps them up to date on taxpayer practices, are the key to an effective system.

A good audit program always includes a continuing educational process for the agents. There must be an awareness of present business practices and patterns of noncompliance. Information must be gathered from every source available and passed on to the agents for use in planning and executing audits.

The evasion patterns discovered in one type of business will usually be found in similar businesses throughout the city, province, or sometimes country because of the associations of businessmen and their tax advisors. Others are peculiar to certain accounting or legal firms. Therefore, a possible part of every audit program could be the quick audit of similar firms when an industry or practitioner pattern becomes known. This improves compliance because it threatens the industry's security--it serves warning that although one company's return may not be selected, if problems are found during the examination of its competitors, it will also be examined.

OFFICE AUDIT PROCEDURES

Office audit is so named because it is performed in the office of the Tax Service, rather than at the taxpayer's premises, and involves those taxpayers whose books and records are simple enough to be readily brought into the office. This type of audit usually includes professionals, wage earners, and some small businesses. In most countries the biggest volumes of tax returns are in this category.

The audits themselves must be "quick" if the sampling of taxpayers is to be large enough to have an impact on compliance. While the actual amount of time spent on these audits will vary according to the laws and customs of each country, the usual range would be from 3 to 4 cases per day to 1 case per day. Quality of auditing is somewhat sacrificed to secure the necessary quantity, as the purpose of audit, in terms of effect, is basically a policing function.

In a normal situation, speed is achieved by the selection committee, during the process of selection, checking the specific items that the auditor should look into. There has always been a matter of professional pride which has the tendency to cause the tax auditor to go beyond these checked items, if permitted. Very strict controls must ensure that this is not done except by special permission.

In developing the system for office audit, the process must include notification of the taxpayer well in advance with a form letter that states in detail what he must bring with him. The interviews must be scheduled to insure that the office auditors have a time deadline and that one taxpayer will be available

for auditing as soon as the previous one is finished.
The supervisor must be readily available for assistance, appeal, and review.

In those countries where the evasion rate is
reasonably low, the selection process itself and the
inspection of the return will give enough base for
the audit. In many countries, however, where the
evasion rate is high the ability both to select returns this way and to get the taxpayer to tell the
truth becomes quite difficult. In those countries,
therefore, it may be preferable to reverse the office
audit selection process.

In the reverse process, studies are made and information secured, by taxpayers, from insurance companies, social clubs, country clubs, expensive auto-
mobile owners, rental paid on property, etc. Using
this list, the taxpayer's return is pulled and the
income shown is compared with the estimated income
necessary to maintain either the general standard of
living shown or the specific income items not reported. It is from an examination of the above that
the taxpayer selection is made and the taxpayer called
in for audit.

In order to effectively handle this technique
the office auditors must be very well trained in in-
terviewing mechanisms and approaches. The facts obtained are not only used in themselves but as a tool
to persuade the taxpayer to divulge all the income
not previously noted on his tax return. The type of
skill needed for this is at a very high level and the
individuals selected for the job should be well
trained and properly recompensed.

Technical Assistance

The technical aspect of the audit function has
as its purpose to improve the quality aspects of tax
practice, both internally and externally. Internally,
it is customary for selected and technically competent
men to quickly review the audits made by field agents,
especially when large cases are involved. This review maintains the quality standards of the agency
and goes far to insure that all taxpayers will be
treated equally. Their decisions and findings are
part of the information that all field agents should
be provided with.

In the event of any questions being raised by them or errors discovered, the case should always be returned to the field office in question for the agent to make the correction.

This function provides official interpretation of laws and regulations in a consistent manner. They should have the potential of transmitting this information not only internally but to tax practitioners and large taxpayers to assist them in abiding by the tax laws. The courtesy, the technical competence, the understanding of these people can create a strong bond of cooperation between the Internal Tax Service and tax practitioner groups.

If it is the custom of the country to license those tax practitioners who are permitted to prepare returns or make appeals, the licensing function is frequently made a responsibility of this technical group. The obvious advantage of the licensing procedure is that it is an immediate and effective weapon against those practitioners whose returns are consistently fraudulent or incompetent.

Taxpayer Assistance

Assistance to the average taxpayer in complying with the tax laws is a very important part of the public image of the tax service. A well-run taxpayer assistance program can bring to the public the concept that the tax service rather than being a part of a "police function" is only interested in the just administration of the law and will go to any lengths to assist the taxpayer in his compliance. While much of the specific planning of taxpayer assistance may well be handled by the Public Information Division, the actual assistance itself is usually considered an audit function. Included in this is general assistance to small taxpayers, the answering of questions in regard to the preparation of tax returns, central telephone points which give this service by telephone for simple questions, evening and lunch-period assistance to those taxpayers who cannot come to the office during the normal business day, availability of tax forms and printed technical instructions at all times, tax returns that are as simple as the law will permit, and all other items that will bring to the public the knowledge that the tax service will do everything possible to help them abide by the tax laws and regulations.

Selection by Data Processing

There has been a trend in a few of the most
developed countries to do the first rough selection
of returns for audit by means of data processing
machinery. This type of selection process would, of
course, be of value only in those countries where the
number of returns filed are too numerous for audit
selection to be made by any manual process.

To select returns by data processing the agency
must have had much experience in the development of
auditing standards by industry, studies of the application of specific standard items in terms of assessments, and item by item studies of which items on the
tax return are more likely to be in error in any particular situation. All this information has to be
fitted into the structure of the country's tax law and
the compliance patterns of the country's taxpayers.

Selection of returns in this manner, therefore,
presupposes an excellent audit system for years that
has developed all the necessary information and used
the information--the ultimate step is only to convert
it to machine language.

The whole question, however, of audit selection
by means of computers, even primary selection, is
still open to some doubts. No country has had that
much experience with the system over a period of time
so that we can say without question this is the goal
towards which all other countries should strive. As
indicated previously, any time a rigid pattern of
selection is used, the pattern becomes known to tax
practitioners and taxpayers; once known, the tax return could be adjusted so that the possibility of
selection is minimized. By the very nature of the
computer, the selection pattern, no matter how sophisticated, must be somewhat rigid. Having tremendous
confidence in the tax practitioners world-wide, I do
believe that any rigid pattern, once known, can be
circumvented.

CHILE'S AUDIT REORGANIZATION

In Chile, when the reorganization and modernization of the tax administration started, the audit
function had little of the systems, methods or techniques discussed previously. In addition, organiza-
tionally there was no central responsibility for the

overall program and procedures. Office audit as a
method did not exist. Most inspectors were bogged
down in paper work, as there was no division between
the paper work and the audit function per se. In
general we can say, therefore, that the installation
of a modern audit function started almost from the
beginning and the changes noted below included all
those that would be necessary for a total restructuring.

The means whereby many of the problems could be
resolved according to previous guidelines were provided for in the reorganization plan for the Chilean
Tax Service which went into effect July 1, 1963. A
new organizational unit, the Departamento Normativo
(Auditing Department), was created in the National
Office to develop auditing standards and techniques
and provide leadership for the audit program. The
audit function was organized in the regions and zones
in such a way as to separate it from the bulk of the
paper processing and enable it to confine itself to
true audit responsibilities. Chiefs of regional and
zone audit were created to carry out national policies
and programs in auditing whereas chiefs of "processing"
with separate staffs were to be responsible for the
bulk of the paper work. An "office of selection" and
"selection committee" were provided for at the zone
level in order to permit selection of cases for audit
on a programmed and more realistic and productive
basis. Audit groups were formed to provide a clear
distinction between field (extensive) and office
(cursory) audit.

The preparation of the organizational structure
that would permit a good audit operation took several
months of thought and discussions. The basic problem
was that the previous organization had the paper work
processing, the bill processing, the technical rulings,
and audit in general all in one bulk. In accordance
with the general principle of management (that the
work that comes to you drives out the work that you
have to go to) inspectors were tied up in handling
taxpayers coming to their offices and other paper
work and had little time left to go to the field.
Office audit, as such, did not exist: the whole audit
function was bogged down.

The present structure of the audit division is
also based on a cultural factor which was taken advantage of. It was impossible five years ago and
difficult today for executives in many cultures to
work horizontally. The concept of people at one

level working voluntarily together to a common end
rather than on instructions from above is a difficult
one. Therefore, to free the audit force as a whole
to work only on audit, a division called "Procesamiento" was created. As indicated by the name, it
handled all paper work, including most of the taxpayer
contacts. The audit function was made into a separate
division consisting of agents and office auditors only,
and at the district level and the branch level both,
i.e. at the operational level, the direct reporting
line was to the Chief of Audit. The first coordinating supervisor was the Zone Administrator. This made
the shift of agents to paper work or taxpayer information difficult except in emergencies.

Experiences during 1962 indicated the necessity
for a technical level in "Procesamiento," somewhere
between a clerk and an agent. This need was filled
by the creation of a new type of job called "Ayudantes
Técnicos" (Technical Assistants). These were secured
by the promotion of the best and most experienced
clerks who were then given a three-month course in the
simple technical knowledge that they needed. Of
course it was a running battle to keep top officials
from making their secretaries "Ayudantes Técnicos" to
get them a salary increase. However, with the help
and the forceful backing of the Director, most of the
Technical Assistants were kept on the work they were
supposed to be doing. In the situation this was quite
good.

Audit standards, procedures, and techniques for
use under the reorganization were incorporated into
Volume III of the Chilean Tax Service Manual by task
forces of Chilean technicians working with the advisor.
The volume was published in June 1963, and has served
as the basis for the audit program since July 1, 1963
and the focal point for the efforts of the new Departamento Normativo (Auditing Department). The volume was
prepared primarily by personnel familiar with general
auditing procedures, but who had little knowledge of
tax auditing procedures. Thus, this volume has been,
and is being, constantly reviewed and amended consistent with tax auditing requirements and the experience
gained in practice in the field.

After the basic Audit Manual, the revisions and
many new systems, including an Agents Handbook, were
developed with the advice of an audit technician.

A pilot project was initiated shortly prior to reorganization to test the usefulness and application in Chile of true office audit practices. In terms of additional taxes, propaganda effect on those taxpayers audited, and needed experience gained from actual working conditions, the pilot program was successful and was the basis for the office audit system in all offices. Using the experience gained during the pilot program, a training course for office auditors was prepared in collaboration with the Training Department of the Service.

The purpose of audit is taxpayer coverage. To develop the proper tax climate, all taxpayers must feel that they may and possibly will be audited. Since staff is always limited, somewhere between 3 per cent to 8 per cent of returns are audited each year, depending on the amount of evasion in the country. To do this amount of auditing and to cover non-business returns, a fast audit of people who can bring their records to the office is necessary. Standards for office audit, depending on the country and its tax laws, would range from 15 to 60 a month against 3 to 5 per month for field audit.

The test program and subsequent visits to local offices proved that office audit had a place in the Chilean Tax Service. However, it also gave evidence that existing procedures required some refinement and improvement. One of these has to do with personal contact at the taxpayer's place of business or residence. This is contrary to usual office audit procedures, but because of the peculiarities of the Chilean taxpayer it became necessary.

Also, in any country where evasion, especially of professionals and small business, is very large, it is useful by surveys of house ownerships, memberships in exclusive clubs, expensive schools, etc., to get possible income information first, and then select the taxpayer for office audit.

Prior to the test program, production goals for office auditors were arbitrarily set at eight closed cases per month. Results obtained from the pilot plan indicated a real possibility of establishing a goal of one case per day. Following review and discussions with the Subdirector Operations and the Chief of the Audit Division, a new standard of 22 cases per month was set. Despite written instructions limiting the

number of items an auditor should examine, the
"auditing in depth" theory of the auditors continued
somewhat to prevail. To combat this, additional instructions were issued making it clear that only
those items (one to three) chosen by the selection
committee are to be audited. The system as now functioning shook down to 16 cases per month and somewhat
more depth than previously.

Considerable time had been devoted to an audit
activity referred to in Chile as "preventive" auditing
Several sections of the Chilean laws require periodic
visits by an inspector from the Service. Some of
these visits are solely for the purpose of establishing tax exemptions (auto assembly plants), others are
to establish quotas, or coefficients of production
(vineyards), others are police actions (distilleries).
In this enforcement area falls the verification of
sales taxes, control of sales of certain assets
(motor vehicles in particular), and the picking up of
delinquent sales tax returns.

From the standpoint of either dollar production
or tax deterrent effect this activity is a losing
proposition. Inspectors are required by Service regulations to make 200 visits each month. An analysis
of dollar production for a 3-month period indicated
a return of as little as 70 pesos (1 cent) per visit
to a high of about 154 pesos. The only real productive area of "preventivo" operations is the verification of sales taxes. This has a twofold impact. The
inspector assesses unreported sales taxes immediately.
The income on which the sales taxes were assessed must
then be recorded as income on the proprietor's books
and thus becomes subject to the tax on business
profits.

It is hoped that preventive audit will eventually
be eliminated. During the last few years the number
of agents doing this work has been cut drastically.
The quick elimination, however, may serve no useful
purposes. To this type of audit there are assigned
those inspectors, some 25 to 30 per cent of the force
who have from a sixth-grade to a high school education
and who do not seem to be competent enough to learn
the necessary skills for either field or office
auditing. If not used in this type of work there is
very little other use for them in the audit structure.
As they retire or leave, however, the policy of the
Service is to replace them with accountants.

Auditing Department
(Departamento Normativo)

This department is the National Office Auditing
Department. Much of the development and work was of
necessity centered around this division. Everything
planned for the audit function, regardless of which
level of activity, is cleared through the Chief of
the Auditing Department.

To assist in getting a quality audit, the following aids have been developed:

   a. A handbook for Audit Group Supervisors--The
       text material used for training Audit Group
       Supervisors it is designed to be the "Bible"
       of the Group Chiefs.
   b. A handbook for Office Auditors.
   c. Guidelines for the Audit Selection Committee.
   d. Review Activity--Guidelines and suggestions.
   e. Visitation Program by Audit Analysts--Sug-
       gestions and outline of topics to be covered.
   f. Guidelines for Evaluation of Work Perfor-
       mance--A program for audit group supervisors.

The Annual Audit Plan

One of the first steps was to establish audit
production goals. In Chile five cases per inspector
per month was established for field audit. Previous
work was approximately that many per year. This os-
tensibly was a goal for each inspector. However, for
planning purposes and control measures it is an average goal for each audit group. (e.g., A group having
eight agents is expected to complete 40 cases per
month.) This point of view had to be taken since
there was not a definite workload distribution by
grade level at the time.

Establishment of goals was only a part of the
Annual Audit Plan (PAF--Plan Anual de Fiscalización).
For the first time the Service had a plan of whom and
when to audit with a national scope, prepared in advance of the work year.

The audit plan was designed to cover an entire
12-month period. However, the original provisional
plan covered the period September 1963 through May
1964. The plan designated as Plan Number 1 covers the
period June 1, 1964 through June 30, 1965. Through
the operation of the provisional plan we were able to

refine the process of developing annual work goals.
As a result of this experience and recommendations
made at a conference of Regional Audit Chiefs, several
dates were changed. A second provisional plan covers
the period July 1, 1965 through December 31, 1965.
Plans designated Number 2 and all subsequent plans
covered the full calendar year, beginning with January 1, 1966. This Annual Audit Plan is now an accepted part of the operation of the Service.

In the Annual Audit Plan the Tax Service sought
to establish definite work goals for each zone, having
as the ultimate aim maximum use of personnel. The
Auditing Department (Departamento Normativo), within
the framework of each annual plan determines the
needs for specialized audits, audits concentrated on
different professional or commercial groups, sample
programs to check economic forecasts, etc.

Three forms have been designed for submitting
plan proposals to the National Office. Form 1 is
prepared at group level and forwarded to the zone.
Form 2 is prepared by the Zone Audit Chief from information shown on the Form 1's. Form 3 is prepared
by the Regional Audit Chief from the Form 2's.

Selection of Cases for Examination

Taxpayer returns selected for examination are
now chosen by a Selection Committee. This group is
called into being once each year shortly after the
newly filed tax returns have been processed. Members
of this group are experienced tax agents who have been
given a brief training course on the selection of
cases.

In prior years the selection of cases for examination was based mainly on the amount of capital
declared by the taxpayer. The Auditing Department
has revised the selection standards to give greater
importance to the net profit and sales.

As a control point a Selection Office has been
created which will function all year long. This
office is responsible for collecting and collating
information on taxpayers, preparing the case control
cards, and in general coordinating the activities of
the Selection Committee.

As selection standards become more accurate industry studies are made, economic studies as to basis

for audit programming are better understood, and
auditing techniques made more skillful, the time
wasted by tax agents will sharply decrease.

Case Control Cards

For years the only control over a case file was
a form which transferred it from the permanent files
to the agent. The serious drawback to this system was
the lack of intermediate controls. Only with the
greatest of difficulty and with much time-consuming
effort could one find a case after it had left the
files. Further, in order to learn what had happened
during and after the audit, several people and many
forms or books had to be consulted.

Meetings were held at which methods were discussed for controlling audit cases during the examination process. The task force and committee members
finally reached substantial agreement on the methods
to be used, and prepared a draft of the essential
features of an audit case control card together with
instructions and flow charts.

This proposed card system consisting of an A, B,
C and D card, was subjected to considerable study by
the full staff of the Auditing Department before being
adopted and made a part of the operating procedures
in the Manual System.

Although these cards were developed for use by
field agents, their use has been made mandatory in
the office audit function as well.

Daily Time Reports

Practical control of an agent's or auditor's time
was not in effect prior to the reorganization. As part
of the office audit pilot program a daily time report
was developed. From this, a daily report grew that
could be used by both agents and office auditors.

After the establishment of an audit production
reporting system it became necessary to make a few
revisions to our time report. While making the necessary changes a time report for the preventive
auditing activity was created.

These new reports were put into effect in April
1964, and have given us the necessary controls as well
as information needed for consolidated reports at the
national level.

Supervision--Audit Groups

Discussions were held with the Training Division relative to expanding the existing course for general supervision to include sessions devoted to the duties and responsibilities of the Audit Group Supervisors. The purpose for having such sessions was to show the supervisors how to do their work with a minimum effort and maximum utilization of time.

A detailed analysis of audit activities had never been made at the supervisory level. To overcome this failure of adequate follow-up of the agent performance, graphs, charts, and tables for discussion were prepared at these training sessions. The charts gave visible evidence of use of time and the production results and were used to great advantage to measure the effectiveness of the agents. All supervisory training for Audit Group Chiefs now include 2 days of specific training on the job of the Group Chief.

Handbook For Revenue Agents

Another first was achieved with the printing of the Agents Handbook. Insofar as we can ascertain this is the first handbook of its kind developed in South America that gives specific guidelines on techniques to be used in auditing various businesses and situations.

Lengthy discussions were held relative to academic knowledge, in-service training, attitudes and the like so that something of specific value to the Chilean agents would be produced; something that could be readily understood by them in their situation.

The handbook was printed in loose-leaf form so that changes could be made easily. The size permits the agent to carry it at all times.

The Office Audit Activity

Prior to the actual reorganization of July 1963, some examinations of taxpayers' records were made by an inspector at this desk in his office. This was auditing in the office. The concept of office audit (mass coverage of taxpayers, one or two item audit, little time spent) was not known.

It was agreed that this concept of a quick "police" audit could have a place in the Chilean enforcement program. To get the program going, a

Pilot Project Office Audit Group was established.   In
May 1963 a group of experienced inspectors were assembled and placed under the jurisdiction of a competent supervisor.

Complete procedure for office audit had not yet
at that time been written. However, the Chilean tax
specialists who were writing the office audit portion
of the audit manual gave briefing sessions to all
auditors and had lengthy sessions with the group
supervisor assigned to the Pilot Project. The audit
advisor worked closely with the Chilean specialist
to make certain that the new concepts were understood.

Using the experience gained during the pilot
program a training course for office auditors was
prepared in collaboration with the Training Division.
Participants in the pilot program were the instructors
for the course. Operating procedures were then incorporated into Volume III of the manual system. Even
though the tax return had been originally chosen for
examination by office auditors procedures for reas-
signing the case to field audit were established
whenever conditions warranted it. The prime condition
for transfer, of course, is reasonable certainty that
an audit in depth will produce considerable additional
revenue or because peculiarities of the taxpayer's
business require a more detailed review.

Taxpayer Assistance Program

The time of the new income tax law. passed in
February 1964, caused much confusion among the taxpaying
public. Therefore, early in March, the Service inaugu-
rated the first determined attempt to provide service to
the public prior to the filing of their tax returns.

In order to be of service to the greatest number
of taxpayers, telephone assistance was established.

Several meetings to get this program rolling were
held by the Chief of the Public Information Division,
an outline for a briefing session for assistors was
developed, a report format designed, and furniture
acquired.

The program was placed in charge of an Audit
Group Supervisor who maintained direct contact with
the technical division so that difficult technical
questions could be answered immediately.

In addition to regular telephone service the
Tax Service has during the filing period, the program
has been augmented by the addition of counters for
the distribution of forms and counters manned by
agents to provide self-help.

Fraud Awareness Seminars

In collaboration with the Intelligence Division,
several seminars were held which were attended by
revenue agents and their supervisors. The purpose
of these seminars was to explain how fraudulent tax
returns are discovered. The subject matter covered
the techniques used in dealing with indications of
fraud. The written outline for these seminars was
used as the basis for writing a chapter on fraud for
the tax agents handbook.

Field Visitations

In Chile there were five Regional Offices, 14
Zone Offices, and 121 Local Offices. In order to
make certain that the audit programs are functioning
properly and that instructions are being followed,
visits were made constantly to these field offices by
the advisor, who was accompanied by an analyst from
the National Office and also by a region or zone audit
representative. They visited every Regional Office,
every Zone Office, with the exception of Punta Arenas,
and some 50 Local Offices. In all 88 separate visits
were made. All other National Office staff on their
visits checked all functions including audit to give
us a constant check on what was "actually" happening.

During the visits all National Office audit staff
took the opportunity to talk to audit group supervisors explaining the how and why of their duties and
responsibilities. They also made certain that the
manual was kept current and being used, discussed
the operation of the Audit Classification Groups,
and questioned as many agents as possible about their
methods of auditing, their relationship with accountants, and their attitude toward taxpayers.

Other Aspects of Audit Assistance

The results of advice and technical assistance
are evident in the end product of major projects.
However, there are day-to-day problems which are resolved and never are directly related to statistical
measurement.

One of the principal duties of an audit analyst is writing instructions in the form of manual issuances and circulars. Discussions were held on the art of writing manuals and prepared written instructions for all writers. A guideline containing 9 points which covered such items as: avoid lengthy sentences, keep to an absolute minimum sentences containing restrictive clauses, write for the reader, etc., was prepared.

Advice was given on how the National Office should control documents containing instructions which originate in Region or Zone Offices. The purpose of this control, of course, is to avoid misinformation or instructions contrary to National Office policy becoming operating standards for field personnel.

Forms always represent problems in that usually more information seems to be required than can possibly appear in a single form. The Organization and Methods Department helped in designing forms for use within the audit activity. The use of standard paragraphs for certain routine reports being prepared by the agents was developed.

As a coordinated effort the Audit Division worked closely with the Intelligence Advisor on the project for matching telephone subscribers with tax rolls. Audit procedures were developed for the canvassing operations as well as the actual audit of the taxpayers involved.

The results of all the above can be seen in the audit assessments that ensued (see Figure 1). In 1962 assessments due to the audit were 32 million Escudos. In 1963 they went to 43 million, 1964 to 103 million, 1965 to 225 million and 1966 to 198 million. The drop in 1966 was caused by the new patrimony law which needed the efforts of most of the inspector force for a 4 to 5 month period. It may be well to note that the great majority of the increase came in the Income Tax area. In 1967 audit assessments rose to 262,765 million.

The Annual Audit Plan, which is now in its fourth year, is completely accepted and the audits are balanced out so as to have the greatest impact on voluntary compliance of the taxpayer. The activity and profits of outside accountants have increased manyfold in this period as corporations and

partnerships have begun to take into consideration
the tax impact of their activities.

The assistance of increased tax revenues in re-
ducing inflation has definitely proved a success although it is difficult to measure it statistically.
If we had estimated a 50 per cent tax evasion rate in
1961, I would estimate an evasion rate of no more than
25 to 30 per cent today. What is more important: the
function has been institutionalized with trained people, planned programs, and a goal. It is hoped and
expected that as time goes on the evasion rate will
be reduced even further.

CHAPTER **8** THE COLLECTIONS
PROCESS

As noted previously, the collection function is
one of the two basic functions of any tax service.
It is this function that collects the taxes, processes
the forms, deposits the payments, and follows up on
delinquent taxpayers.

ELEMENTS OF THE PROCESS

1. The maintenance of the current accounts,
i.e. a record of filing for every taxpayer of his payments each year and other key identifying information
necessary to follow up on the amounts still due to the
government or credits which are owing.
Up to comparably recent times this was a tremendous clerical job involving thousands of people in
each of the various countries. Today, most countries
of any size put these accounts on data processing
machinery which does the job much more accurately and
efficiently and much faster. This leaves the personnel and money available for those activities which
cannot be computerized.

2. This function also receives and processes the
tax returns that are filed and either deposits the
remittances or maintains a check on the deposits if
made in banks or in Treasury offices. In most countries this is still done by hand. As more experience
is gained, the accounting for the remittances, or the
verification of the remittances paid, are being computerized. (This is usually the second step in the
computerization of the function.)

3. In those countries whose system permits the
payment of refunds, this is the function which checks
on the validity of the refund and issues the payments
either directly or again through computerization.

4. As part of the general accounting responsibility, it is normal for sales and accounting of

99

excise tax stamps, licenses, or any other tax income
item to be controlled by this accounting function.

5.   To complete the collection process, this
function is always responsible for the collection of
delinquent accounts and the securing of delinquent
returns.
      The above two functions are put together, in
that the type of personnel used for the collection of
delinquent accounts (amounts of money declared and not
paid on time) and the techniques used to make these
collections are of very similar nature to the canvassing or other methods used for the securing of
delinquent returns (taxpayers who do not file).

      As is obvious, the first four points are accoun-
ting and processing functions whose major problems
are the tremendous volume, and the detail within this
volume, that must be maintained currently and accurately. Fortunately, as noted above, the process
lends itself to the use of equipment, either by data
processing, bookkeeping, or various other accounting
machines and techniques. The very large scale of its
operation causes a tremendous use of personnel time
for taxpayer contact and routine correspondence. Work
simplification programs are useful in keeping this to
a minimum.

      The computerization of the accounting procedure
undoubtedly is more effective than manual work. Two
problems are encountered, however: one is that an inefficient manual system, if continued, is also an
inefficient computer system; it is the system that
counts, not the method of doing it. The second one
is that in a country where unemployment is very great
and the number of taxpayers small (under 1 million),
it is questionable whether the tremendous cost of the
rental of computers could not be put to better advantage in the payment of salaries.

      The collection of delinquent accounts is facili-
tated through the tax service having the authority of
seizure, auction, levy, and other legal enforcement
tools to force a taxpayer, after persuasion has failed,
to pay his debts. Consistently, the amount of enforcement authority that actually has to be used is
very minor, if available. In 99 per cent of the cases,
the taxpayer pays before the auction or the levy as
long as he is sure they are being carried through.
It is because of this that most forward-looking
countries have permitted these actions to be taken
administratively. This is not only a less costly way

of doing it, by far, but since there is always appeal
to the courts, a just way also. The key point here
is that if the tax service has the authority it will
very rarely have to use it.

In those cases where the tax service has to go
through judicial process to get this authority, there
is a tendency to keep the courts very busy on routine
matters to the detriment of other important matters.
This, at the same time, enables the taxpayer to evade
his tax debts for so long a time that, if the economy
is at all inflationary, the actual return to the
Treasury is very small.

In the actual carrying out of the delinquent returns function, assuming it is properly programmed, a
number of contacts will have to be made preliminarily.
This is to make sure the taxpayer has all the opportunity possible to pay his debt before any action is
taken. There are definite time intervals, therefore,
when the tax inspector is free and is in specific
areas of the city. This is the time that is usually
made available for the canvassing of delinquent returns on a geographic, industrial, or some other predetermined basis. The type of staff used and the
technique used in both functions noted is quite
similar.

Government policy in the collections area, the
percentage of part-payment agreements and the methods
of collection are so diverse that no guidelines could
cover the needs of any individual country.

REORGANIZATION OF THE
COLLECTIONS FUNCTION

The changes in the collection function in Chile,
and how they were accomplished, constitute the example
of a country which has its collection and audit function in separate agencies of government.

Tax administration in the Government of Chile in
1963 was divided between the Internal Tax Service, the
Treasurer of Chile, and the Legal Collections Division.
The first two belong to the Treasury Department and the
last to the Council for the Defense of the State which
was under the Department of Justice. Internal Tax
Service handled all problems relating to the receipt
and examination of tax returns, obtaining returns when
they were not filed voluntarily, prosecuting tax

declaration frauds, and hearing tax claims and sending
bills.   The Treasurer received all tax payments and
referred to Legal Collections all delinquent tax accounts.   The latter agency collected them under a
judicial procedure for collection provided by Chilean
laws.   Although both Treasury and Legal Collections
were authorized to collect some delinquent taxes administratively, neither had been doing so.

In April 1963, as part of the studies of the Internal Tax Service, contact was made with the Treasury
in order to find out what proportion of the assessments
made by the Audit Division were actually collected and
what relationship this bore to the total amount of
taxes collected.   Two meetings with key Treasury officials produced evidence that the way their figures
were kept it was impossible not only to determine the
assessments collected but even the assessments made.
Obviously, there was no point in improving the organization and systems of the Internal Tax Service to
bring in additional revenue if the money was not actually collected and therefore usable.

The first step was to try and get some reliable
statistics as to how much money was really owed and
who owed the money, by tax and by amount, and by date.
Approximately 30 to 40 men in the Legal Collection
Division worked four months in compiling a series of
charts which for the first time put into the hands of
responsible officials the information necessary to
make a plan.

Activites

A thorough investigation was made of the organization of Legal Collection, its relations with the
Treasury and the Chilean Tax Service, and its actual
operation both in the field and in headquarters.   As
part of this, visits were made to many field offices
throughout the country and conversations were held
with personnel in the National Office and with employee groups.   Studies were made of available records
and the legal framework under which the collection
activities are conducted.   These detailed studies
produced the factual basis for the changes.   There is
no substitute for personal on-site investigations.

As a result of these studies, proposals were
jointly formulated by the Legal Collection Division
and the Secretary of Treasury for a complete revision
of the organizational structure, the laws relating to

outstanding taxes, the methods of collection, and the transfer of the staff or Legal Collection into the government service.

As an outgrowth of these proposals, a top-level Presidential Commission was officially appointed to study the problem and advise on the improvement of the tax collection structure and law. The Chairman of the Commission was the Treasurer General. His principal assistants, who advised on the problem, were the Director of the Legal Collections, a top lawyer from the Justice Department, and an outside expert on collection of delinquent accounts. Legislative changes were included in the proposed new constitution and in general normative law which the administration submitted to the Congress while the Commission was still sitting.

In thus anticipating the Commission's decision the attempt was made to avoid the certain delays in the legislative process. While many legislative problems arose and the law was rejected twice, it was finally passed in January 1967, the first Administrative Collection Law in South America. The full regulations were published in September 1968.

The Commission completed its preliminary work in January 1966 and sent to the President its final report, which was an improved version of the previous recommendations. Acceptance of the report was secured and the Treasurer of Chile, who now heads the Legal Collections function, is implementing the recommendations.

A draft of a detailed manual of procedure for the new collection system, including drafts of the forms to be used, was prepared during this time.

Details of Work

Investigation showed that the old system of collecting delinquent taxes was not effective, was inequitable, and was not able to fulfill its assigned functions. This was due to a number of factors, principal among them being that it was based upon a system whereby the tax collectors worked on commission and these commissions were note even directly related to the amount collected. The entire system provided the collectors with substantial remuneration for a small amount of work, and any desirable measures for improvement which impinged upon these commissions

were resisted.   There was, furthermore, no control
over the men and their work since their supervisors
were attorneys who devoted only a minimum amount of
time to the office.   In addition, there were a number
of legal impediments to effective collection.   The
commission-oriented judicial collection system could
not cope with the necessity for a volume collection
operation which had a total of outstanding liabilities increasing almost 100 per cent a year.

The recommendations presented called for an end
to the then mode of operation and remuneration and
for a complete restructuring of the agency.   Furthermore, the recommendations called for the merger of
Legal Collections with the Treasury to effect econo-
mies of operation and simplification of procedure and
for a number of legal changes in collection procedure.
This was to provide the country with a systematic
high-volume program for collecting established liabilities.

The Communal Treasurer, where 50 per cent or more
of all delinquent accounts should be collected, was
made the first step in a simplified administrative
volume collection process.   The necessity of the more
time-consuming and ponderous enforcement efforts of
Legal Collection was kept for the more difficult
cases.   The whole approach was to change the role of
Collections from a mere collection agency to that of a
collection enforcement agency which would encourage
voluntary payment into the Treasury offices.   Furthermore, the Treasury would use its data processing machines to prepare the account assemblies which would
be used successively by the Communal Treasurer and
Legal Collection to manage their operations.   The
latter would use the cashiers of the former to avoid
the additional accounting.   The mails and telephones
would be used for initial demands and the collection
officers of Legal Collections would become the experts
in ferreting out assets and enforcing difficult collection.

Needless to say, these recommendations met opposition from those employees in Legal Collection who
would lose their sinecures and from Legal Collection
headquarters, which was reluctant to oppose these employees and feared the merger with Treasury.   Cooperation was received from Legal Collection on the fact-
finding level, but it was unproductive to work with
them in any attempt to make basic improvements.   An
attempt at a pilot project embodying a number of
changes met difficulties.

The recommendations for the complete change of organization, salaries, systems, etc., did receive the whole-hearted approval of the new administration the Treasurer General, the Secretary of Treasury, and the President. Accordingly, the work went forward, principally with the Treasurer and his staff, to have the government accept and submit the legislative changes necessary to effectuate the recommendations. Also, the government appointed the commission whose recommendations followed and improved the recommended changes and which supervised the procedure.

The Treasury Department's mechanized accounting system is operating the administrative collection process as well as producing the necessary forms for collection enforcement. The forms are being programmed and notices of delinquency are being mailed. A program for administrative collection work has also been put into effect.

In addition, a constitutional amendment limiting the power to initiate condonation laws to the executive has passed the Chamber of Deputies and is being considered by the Senate. These condonation laws which have been passed regularly for the last few years by the Congress reduce all interest and penalties on unpaid taxes and permit delays in payment, thus removing all incentive to pay timely or otherwise comply with the tax laws. Some legislative delay will be unavoidable, but the shift of the total collection function to the Treasury improved volume collection under present laws and prepared the way for implementation of the legislative changes.

The acceptance of the Presidential Commission's recommendations and the continued existence of that Commission has made implementation easier. The Treasury has expanded its existing data processing pilot project into a total collection project and are assisting the effectuation in the entire country. This includes the training of front-line personnel and supervisors, the preparing of official manuals, and all the myriad details to set a new organization going.

It became evident in the work with the Treasurer that there should be more coordination of effort and machine operation between it and the Internal Tax Service. Preliminary discussions of the need to realign the Treasurer's and the Internal Tax Service

operations have taken place. This will be the necessary next step after the merger of Legal Collection
and the Treasury and the implementation of the legislation on administrative collections.

(Appendix E contains the section headings of the
material jointly developed for the reorganization of
Legal Collection and a copy of the new law.)

CHAPTER **9** THE USE OF
DATA PROCESSING

As indicated previously in the chapter on collections, a computer system is only as good as the
basic operating system itself. A poor operating system and method, when programmed in computer terms and
done with the speed of the computer, merely increases
the speed but not the efficiency of the system. In
installing a computer, therefore, one starts with a
complete study of the tax system not only in terms of
readjusting it to fit a computer but readjusting it
into a more effective system. It is during this process that the computer needs are determined. One always works from the system to the computer and never
from the computer back to the system.

The contribution to good tax administration that
a carefully planned and efficiently run data processing installation can make justifies the interest of
administrators everywhere. But the very complexity
of making such an installation together with some
problems which are unique (at least in magnitude) requires a commitment by the tax agency that must be
carefully considered. It is frequently the failure
to understand the magnitude of this commitment, and
the impact the system will have on the agency and
the public alike, or the failure to follow through
with the detailed planning required, that magnifies
all the problems. This may plague the agency for
years.

SETTING UP A COMPUTER SYSTEM

In the early stages of considering the conversion
of a manual tax processing system to a computerized
system, the tax administrator will have his only opportunity to decide objectively whether his agency
really needs a computer. In many cases, he will discover that he can obtain many of the benefits of computerization (through optimizing his manual system)
without incurring the disadvantages which may apply.

107

Once the decision is made, no matter how frustrated
he may become later at the apparent unworkability of
his system, he is wedded to it. In recent times,
there are almost no reported cases of computerized
systems once started being abandoned.

A feasibility study is normally the first step.
This is conducted by fairly high-ranking representatives of operating segments of the agency and has the
responsibility of determining the objectives of the
system, the benefits and disadvantages involved, and
the cost comparison to the existing system. In addition to the policy, legal, and technical questions
normally involved, some special considerations may
apply in certain countries.

The feasibility study is the opportunity to make
the full determination whether to computerize and to
set out the broad outline of the system. The objective evaluation of the proposal to install a computer
or to convert an existing system to a larger or newer
model, occurs during this rather detailed study.

The major problem area of computerizing, outside
of a very few well-developed countries, is the problem
of what, in computer language is called the software,
i.e. trained personnel. The problems, generally
speaking, are:

1. The difficulties of securing highly qualified
systems analysts, programmers, and machine operators in
the numbers required. Lack of them causes ineffective
operations and high rental expenses during the period
which the computer should be operating at capacity.
2. Qualified computer personnel (systems analysts, programmers, and operators) are difficult to
retain on most government salary scales. Lengthy and
continuous training classes are required to maintain
staff lost to private business.
3. All of the most recent technical literature,
including operator handbooks and programmer instruction manuals, are in English and have not been trans-
lated.
4. If there is a large segment of unemployed or
underemployed in the country, the social costs of re-
placing them by a machine must be considered.

In addition, two other major considerations are
the maintenance service available and the postal system. Computers are delicate machines and must be
housed in air-conditioned rooms whose temperatures

cannot vary. The availability of spare parts, which
are usually imported, and the availability of competent technicians and equipment in the air-conditioning
field are extremely important. If they are not available, the whole system can break down because the key
portion of it done by the computer is not operable.

Most computer systems rely heavily, also, on the
country's postal system. If the mail system is not
reliable to the point where the tax service and the
courts can legally assume that any envelope mailed
will be delivered, a heavy burden is placed on the
entire system.

During the feasibility study, the team members--
being knowledgeable in tax processes--may conclude
that the proposed equipment is not necessary and that
the increased production or savings of considerable
magnitude can be obtained by optimizing manual processes and making them more efficient. The study
phase is essential to installing computer systems in
any case.

If computerization is found to be advantageous,
a more detailed study is required in order to develop
data for submission to manufacturers for contract bids.
This data includes brief descriptions of the projects
or applications to be computerized, diagrams of work
flow, data on work volume, man-hour costs, etc.

In the selection of specific equipment needed,
the talents of experienced computer systems analysts
are required. The careful analysis of all existing
procedures, policies and objectives provide the foun-
dation upon which the new system will be built.

It is at this point that advice is needed to secure a computer most suited to the general system that
is being developed. It is at this key point where it
is suggested that outside advice be secured. While
the companies concerned will usually recommend the
most suitable machine that they make, it requires good
expertise to make the decision as to which company
produces the best machine for the purposes. Most important is the decision as to what adjustments or
additions may be needed specifically in order that
the system be carried out with the greatest effectiveness.

The longest lead time required in installation
planning is for the recruitment and training of the

specialized personnel required. Tax administrators
will usually find a dearth of these people--particu-
larly systems analysts and programmers--at salaries
they can afford to pay and must then train them themselves. These analysts and programmers must design
and install the system before the computers can operate. Later on, less skilled technical personnel must
be trained: computer operators, magnetic tape libra-
rians, key-punch operators.

Planning and scheduling of construction and delivery of physical facilities and equipment follows.
This includes layout of the computer room and tape
library, increased air conditioning, electrical power
requirements, not only for the computer but for all
the supporting equipment such as key-punch machines,
false floors, remodelling to improve work flow, specialized shelving in the tape library and in other
work areas, computer generated accounting records, etc.

During the design and programming for the actual
tax processing system, additional procedures also must
be designed (and some computerized) for the management
and control of the computer system. These include a
procedure for scheduling and controlling production
as work flows through the organization from the time
it is received until it is completely processed.
Another procedure is required for scheduling the most
efficient use of the computer itself (a comparatively
huge expense). Still another is a well thought-out
system for the computer tape library to insure that
the hundreds or thousands of reels of tape on hand are
not lost, misplaced, or the data on them accidentally
destroyed.

In all of the foregoing, the selected computer
manufacturer will normally offer advice and a certain
amount of technical assistance. They all offer training for programmers, machine operators, and sometimes
a few courses for analysts. They also offer some systems design and programming support and advice on physical installation. The bulk of the work, however,
and all the responsibility will fall on the tax agency.
It is appealing but dangerous to rely too heavily on
the manufacturer's representatives for too much support.

One of the biggest problems with first buying a
computer and then developing a system is that the
computer tends to become a printing machine rather
than a part of the operation. It prints taxpayer

lists, taxpayer delinquents, etc. This, of course,
can be done more cheaply without having a computer.

The modern computer systems design for tax agencies takes full advantage of today's computers by
establishing as the heart of the system a master file
of taxpayers. This master file usually carries all
of the pertinent data on each taxpayer: identifying
by a carefully constructed number his liability for
various types of taxes, his total tax liability, any
arrangements for part-payments, a record of his payments, etc. In addition, the file carries summary
accounting and statistical data for all taxpayers.
With this comprehensive, centralized set of records,
the system can not only run the accounting system of
the tax service but pull out specific taxpayers for
delinquencies, make a rough selection for audit, issue
bills, and account for payments, etc. It should be
the central core of the collection process. The computer is an operating tool, not a printing press or
a method of making economic studies.

The computer can check the master file to identify taxpayers who have failed to file tax returns or
who have failed to make payments and generate delinquency notices. It can assess penalties and compute
interest and generate bills. It can produce name and
address slips for mailing tax returns. It can produce
transcripts or excerpts of the taxpayer's account.
And finally, it can generate accounting, financial,
and statistical reports of all types from this mass
of data.

Tax agencies should prepare themselves and the
general public for critical periods in computerizing
their processing system: the period of actual conversion from existing manual processing to the newly
designed system. News of the mere existence of a
computer in the tax agency has a marked enforcement
impact on the taxpaying public. The operating segments of the agency itself will feel the impact even
more strongly. Careful planning and follow-through
and indoctrination throughout the agency will help
minimize the inevitable confusion, errors, delays,
frustrations, and complaints during the transition.
One of the most helpful things in this regard is to
insure that the computerized processing system be
thoroughly documented to an unbelievably detailed degree, with complete instructions for all who are involved in the system. Computerized data processing
cannot tolerate ambiguity or lack of uniformity in

its input, and a carefully organized body of instructions in handy manual form is essential for smooth
installation, conversion, and operation.

THE CHILEAN EXPERIENCE

In Chile the Internal Tax Service had used mechanical processing equipment previously for 30 years,
having first installed punched card machines about
1935 for the centralized production of tax rolls and
bills. The agency in 1962 had just accepted a proposal of International Business Machines and had contracted with that company for the installation of two
fairly small Type 1401 computers. The equipment was
installed and put into operation in the middle of
1963. Since that time the complement of equipment of
the Internal Tax Service has been the same except that
in August 1966, a faster model tape drive was substi-
tuted.

This equipment, with substantial data processing
capacity, had been used almost entirely for the same
purposes as were the punched card machines it replaced; i.e. the preparation of tax rolls (printed
lists of all returns filed) and tax bills.

A few of the top officials of the Internal Tax
Service were aware that the equipment could be much
more valuable if used for correlation, consolidation,
and analysis of tax information than when used primarily for printing, but they could not raise the
efficiency of operation of the Machine Department up
to a level that allowed machine and employee time for
more fruitful applications. They recognized the need
for help, and in the middle of 1965 a data processing
specialist was contracted with for a two-year tour
with two principal purposes: first, to observe the
day-to-day operations of the Machine Department and
suggest ways of improving its efficiency to the point
where its assigned tasks could be carried out in an
orderly, timely, and accurate manner; and second, to
study the data processing requirements of Chile's tax
system, devise a long-range plan for the handling,
use and storage of tax data, and get the local

officials started in the execution of the plan. These
two efforts are discussed under separate headings
below.

Operational Efficiency

There was unanimous dissatisfaction of National
Office and field officials and employees with the
service provided by the Machine Department. The complaints were the same everywhere: work was completed
late and with many errors. Upper-echelon National
Office officials expressed frustration, in addition,
at the Department's inability to take on other work
they felt it should do. Observation of the Department
itself showed the absence of any effective work planning, scheduling, or production standards, a lack of
discipline, and unwillingness of low-level supervisors
to assume responsibility.

Eventually it became obvious that a new Chief of
the Machine Department was the first step to the solution to the problem of making that organization an
effective element, but the difficulty of finding an
adequate replacement, together with the extreme
rigidity of the government employment system prevent-
ed the change for a year.

The problem of getting a competent and cooperative advisor to a new chief of the Data Processing
Division was a difficult one. First was finding
such a man in Chile, as possibly such a man did not
exist. An Office Manager for Philips Electric and
a former employee of IBM was finally located. During
two meetings a tentative agreement was reached that
he would take the job.

He took over the management of the Machine Department in April 1966, and the change in productivity
and atmosphere was soon apparent. The new Chief was
competent, he gained the respect of the employees, and
the rise in production levels and accuracy has been
evident in the disappearing backlogs of work. A system of work planning, scheduling, and control and a
performance measurement system has been developed.
Other key measures noted previously are in process.

A New Tax Data
Processing System

A thorough study was made of the way the Internal
Tax Service receives, handles and uses information
relevant to internal taxes. Information handling
methods and techniques are only a subsidiary function,
or service, in the administration of a tax system;
nevertheless, they have an extremely important bearing
on the effectiveness and cost of tax collection.

A particularly strong argument in favor of auto-
mation of tax information processing is that it permits a higher degree of centralization of clerical
operations. Another factor is that it is difficult
to do by hand the volumes of routine steps which
available and economically feasible equipment can do.

In early December 1965, a comprehensive proposal
for the complete overhaul of the government's tax
accounting and processing systems was presented together with a recommendation that the Minister of
Finance direct the completion of a detailed study and
the development of the specific system. The key to
the proposal made is the assembly in one place, in
form readable by a computer, of all the necessary information about each taxpayer (master file). Only in
this way is it possible to make use of the data involving each entity which pays, or should pay, taxes.

Both the Director of the Chilean Tax Service and
the Treasurer General favored the plan and, with very
slight modification, they jointly submitted it to the
Minister of Finance. The Minister indicated his approval by issuing in March 1966, a decree ordering
the recommended study to be made and naming the officials who must oversee it and make the detailed
official recommendation.

The initial report was made to the Minister in
early January 1967. The data processing advisor had
for some months spent the major portion of his time
with the task force of technicians of the agencies
involved and, although the design of the system was
not yet complete, the principal elements were clear:

1. The Internal Tax Service was scheduled to establish a permanent and continuing file, on magnetic
tape, which identifies each income taxpayer by his
name and national carnet number.

TABLE 3

Data Processing Equipment
in Machine Department
(all IBM)

Conventional punched card equipment

No.	Machine Name	Model
23	Alphabetic key punch	026
12	Alphabetic key verifier	056
1	Sorter	083
1	Numeric collator	088
1	Accounting machine	407
1	Reproducer	519
1	Interpreter	552

Electronic computing equipment

No.	Machine Name	Model
2	Central processor	1401
2	Printer	1404
2	Card reader-punch	1402
2	Auxiliary memory	1406
2	Auxiliary console	1407
10	Magnetic tape units	7330

2.   All income tax returns would be recorded as
transactions in the file, and there would be added
account for each taxpayer who files returns for other
kinds of taxes but does not file an income tax return.
3.   There would be a comparison of information
reported by taxpayers with other data received from
independent sources; for example, income tax with-
holding agents, and local governments which register
motor vehicles. There would also begin the mechanical
application of criteria for various study purposes.
4.   In 1970 and later years, it was proposed to
add other kinds of data which have direct connection
with internal taxes, such as imports, travel abroad,
foreign exchange transactions.

The Minister of Finance approved the plan and
ordered the execution to start. The data-processing
advisor concentrated his efforts upon the training of
managers and technicians in the parts they must play
in the long and arduously detailed development and
preparation of the installation of the system.

The work of development and testing will necessarily continue for several years, but the good grasp
of the essentials of the idea shown by the principal
officials concerned, together with the warm support
of those who have thus far been involved at every
level, justifies the expectation that Chile will be
able to modernize its handling of tax information with
benefits to the revenues.

The list of machines used are shown in Table 3.

CHAPTER **10** THE TAX FRAUD
DIVISION

If we go back to the purposes of tax administration, i.e. to create a climate of compliance, then a
Tax Fraud Division is a very important factor.   The
cost of this Division is usually much more than any
money it will collect.   Its impact on voluntary compliance, however, is tremendous.

OBJECTIVES OF THE DIVISION

The objective of a Fraud Division is not per se
to enforce the criminal statutes of the law or to
prosecute those taxpayers who commit tax fraud, but
to create a spectre of jail and disgrace for those who
constantly evade their just and legal share of the tax
burden.   This function, more than any other, depends
on intelligent and capably presented publicity.   The
selection of type of cases, the time of prosecution,
the date of sentencing, and the reasons for prosecution are all in themselves more important than the
actual prosecution itself.

There is a general feeling in countries where
evasion is high and no Fraud Division exists that "we
cannot put the whole country in jail."   This is, of
course, setting up a straw man that does not exist.
For example, in the U.S., where there has been the
greatest development of fraud activity, there is a
staff of 1,731 technicians.   In 1967, there were 9,309
preliminary investigations; of these 3,193 became
full-scale investigations, prosecution was recommended
in 2,015 cases; 1,074 taxpayers were actually brought
to trial, 582 were convicted or pleaded guilty, and a
large portion of the 582 were set free without any
time in jail.   This number must be compared against
the 107 million tax returns filed.   Despite this very
small example, the fear of jail sentences creates an
evasion ceiling which very few taxpayers try to pene-
trate.

As in the auditing of tax returns, the cases for tax fraud must be carefully selected by industry, geography, and economic groups. Jail sentences and convictions should be timed for the three- or four-month period before the taxpayer ordinarily files his return. The investigative technique of checking bills and invoices and other items of evidence in itself disseminates the news of a fraud check.

In initiating a Tax Fraud Division the usual technique is to select as first cases those individuals or corporations whom the general public would be willing to accept worthy of jail, irrespective of whether they have filed fraudulent tax returns or not. This is an important point in the acceptance of the whole approach that tax fraud should be punished by jail sentences. A famous example of this is the Al Capone case in the U.S., which really initiated the Fraud Division, and which was acceptable because of public belief that Capone's activities should be stopped.

The inception of an operating and effective Fraud Division in Chile was one of the main causes of the startling increase in their tax intake. Chile, which is under the Latin system of justice, has jailed less than five taxpayers in the last four years. However, well over 100 have served some time in preventive custody. The impact here was much greater than in the U.S. because of the public belief that you could not put people in jail for tax evasion in South America.

Jail sentences for fraud can be put into operation anywhere if intelligently approached. When the tax service has the authority to act and acts efficiently, the number of taxpayers personally and directly affected is extremely small.

The fraud function is basically part of the audit function and should get the majority of its cases by direct referral from the audit function. The Audit Division takes care of those taxpayers who are reasonably honest. The definition of "reasonably" would vary from country to country. All countries, however, have a point of agreement, some point that a majority will accept--that certain taxpayers are blatantly dishonest and have gone too far. These taxpayers are taken care of by the Fraud Division.

In the following pages, which indicate how this approach was applied to Chile, training is emphasized time and time again. A fraud inspector must not only

know accounting but also a considerable amount of law.
The evidence he unearths must stand up in court. He
must learn all the usual means of evading taxes and
be an expert on finding them. The general investigative techniques and the techniques of interrogating
people should be taught in the way they are taught in
police academies. Above all, the staff must include
people of imagination who will go forward of their own
accord without waiting detailed direction. It usually
takes a minimum of one year for reasonable training,
both in classroom and on the job, to qualify a fraud
inspector.

DEVELOPMENT OF THE CHILEAN
TAX FRAUD DIVISION

One of the first divisions established, after the
training school, was a Fraud Division. It is a function basic to compliance. The fear of jail has greater
impact in South America than in the U.S. in that inflation negates the effects of fines and the jails
lack modern comforts.

Chile in 1961 had a tax fraud law, but it had
never been used, for lack of trained staff, a positive
administrative approach, and legislative approval of
such a division in the Internal Tax Service. During
the fifteen months of 1962-63, with the help of an
expert in the function, a Division of 49 trained men
was created, practiced on sample cases, and was ready
to go full force in July 1963, when the changes in
the Organic Law set up the Division legally. The new
Organic Statute provided for the creation of a tax
enforcement unit, whose function was to be:

1.   The investigation of tax fraud cases.
2.   The recommending and initiation of prosecution of tax evaders before ordinary justice when vio-
lation can be penalized with corporal punishment.
3.   Active participation by the Tax Service in
the development of a criminal prosecution when the
respective action is presented by the Chilean Tax
Service, or to help in the presentation of evidence
when the action is presented by the Government Defense
Council at the request of the Director of the Tax
Service.

During the interim period between September 1961,
and July 1963, the Director of the Chilean Tax Service
administratively created an Intelligence Division
within the Service as an operating office charged with

the responsibility of seeking out areas of tax fraud,
of identifying subjects for investigation, of gathering evidence through investigative procedures, and of
preparing cases for criminal prosecution. This administrative order was issued on December 21, 1961,
and the operational phase of the work began soon
thereafter. Initially 49 people were selected to
staff this Division. The personnel consisted of 8
attorneys, 7 inspector supervisors, 18 inspectors, and
16 clerks, typists and porters. Two additional attorneys were assigned by the Legal Department to service
with the Intelligence Division in an advisory capacity.
The personnel was increased to a total of 71 within
a year and consisted entirely of investigating agents
and supporting clerical personnel.

Since there was no previous experience with this
function and since complete acceptance had not been
achieved, an attempt was made to use this new division
as a dumping ground for unwanted personnel. After
much discussion and heated argument, a partial agreement was achieved and a concerted effort was made to
recruit the best talent available within the Chilean
Tax Service. Employees were sought who had the potential for tax enforcement work. All technical personnel
were carefully screened and selected on the basis of
their educational, professional, and experience back-
grounds.

Ten of the group selected were sent to the United
States to study the overall structure, techniques and
method of operation of the U.S. intelligence system.
The group left for the United States in December 1961,
and returned to Chile in March 1962.

While the group was in the U.S., the remaining
personnel, working under advisorship, attempted to
organize and develop the Intelligence Division and to
begin operations with the investigation of potential
tax fraud cases.

Upon the return of the group from the United
States, a single force began working toward the execution of the goals set by the Chilean Tax Service.

Orientation Training

It was recognized at the outset that it would be
necessary to train a force of highly skilled agents,
supervisors and attorneys if the new unit was to carry
out its assigned role. Accordingly, a sixfold training
program was developed as follows:

1. Orientation training.
2. Training in the United States.
3. Basic classroom training of special agents.
4. On-the-job training.
5. Training of staff through departmental
    meetings.
6. In-service training for other than Intelli-
    gence Division personnel.

The orientation training was designed to acquaint
the selected staff with the proposed program for Chile
and to orient the groups preparing to leave for the
United States. The program was introduced by the
Director of the Chilean Tax Service, who also presented a program which he felt would accomplish the
needs. Subsequently, members of other groups who had
visited the United States as observers or on training
tours spoke to the group on their experiences. Other
areas covered during this training session included
the following subjects:

1. Organization and function of the United
    States Internal Revenue Service.
2. Jurisdiction organization and policy of the
    Intelligence Division.
3. Methods of operation.
4. Duties, responsibilities and qualifications
    of the intelligence agent.
5. Origins of investigations.
6. Investigation techniques.
7. Law and evidence.
8. Processing of cases.
9. Examples of cases successfully prosecuted in
    the United States.
10. Study of Chilean laws and regulations.
11. Case studies of tax frauds in Chile.

All training sessions were conducted on a seminar
basis. Classroom participation was excellent and en-
thusiasm ran high. The training provided within the
United States changed the concept of general training
heretofore to specialized training.

The U.S. training was divided into two phases:
a general orientation of the United States tax system,
and a concentrated study of the function and operation
of the United States Intelligence Division.

Although the agents selected for the actual work
of investigating tax evaders were men of audit experience, the fact remained that they had to be indoctri-
nated into the specialized work they were selected to

perform.   A ten-point crash program of training was
designed to provide these experienced agents with the
fundamentals required of a well-rounded tax-investi-
gator and to apply corrective measures to investigative and procedural shortcomings recognized in the
early stages of the operation.

The course consisted of 35 sessions of 1 1/2
hours.   One session was given each day.   Training was
limited, in the daily schedule, so that agents could
continue to devote the major portion of their work-
day to actual case work.   The subjects covered included topics such as: mission of the Intelligence
Division; the Tax Code; revenue violations; rules of
evidence; investigation techniques; tax felonies;
criminal procedures; auditing; and administrative
procedures.

Basic training was supplemented by on-the-job
training.   As part of the on-the-job training program,
the "buddy" system was employed in the development and
investigation of a tax fraud case.   In this system the
more experienced agents were teamed up with agents
of lesser experience.   Case assignments were made on
a selected basis to the two-man team.   As the inex-
perienced agent gained investigative know-how he was
assigned cases of his own and eventually used in a
training capacity with other newly recruited agents.
The work of the "buddy" system was under the close
supervision of the group supervisors who provided
continuous guidance and regular case reviews.

Training was also provided at regular staff
meetings.   This training was designed primarily to
develop the basic knowledge of the top staff members,
such as group supervisors, Division Chiefs and the
Assistant Division Chiefs.   At these meetings
a review was conducted of the work performed and
discussions were held concerning problems involved
in cases.   This meeting acted as a trial and jury for
cases in which criminal prosecution had been recommended by the special agents.   The case under discussion was studied by a "Prosecuting Attorney" and a
"Devil's Advocate."   Both parties presented their
arguments and a conclusion was reached to the effect
that further investigation was necessary, that the
case merited immediate prosecution, or that the case
should not be undertaken.   The entire proceedings
were tape-recorded for later use by the agents and
for future training sessions.

Visits were made to field offices to stimulate the identification of fraud cases in the zones outside the Santiago population area where the initial work of the Department was being concentrated. These visits explained the procedure for the referral of cases to the Intelligence Department when indications of fraud were discovered and how to discover those indications. In the Zone Offices, meetings were scheduled with top management personnel, field supervisory personnel, and all field inspectors that could be reasonably brought to the Zone Office. In those instances where distance prohibited the bringing in of all audit personnel, the group supervisors who attended the meeting carried the message back to those not attending. Wherever possible, meetings were held with local business and professional groups concerning the Chilean Tax Service's enforcement program.

Regular press releases were sent to the leading newspapers. Radio and newsreel coverage was also secured at the time of the signing of the papers instituting Chile's first tax evasion case in which criminal action was taken.

Tax Fraud Projects

During this initial period, work was also begun on the following projects:

1. The initiation of a comprehensive survey of all criminal aspects of the law that affects the intelligence operation. Lawyers of the Chilean tax team drafted a complete legislative program that would facilitate intelligence operations and the prosecution of tax cases through the courts.
2. An executive decree of the President of Chile was issued requiring all departments of the Government of Chile to cooperate with and furnish information to the Chilean Tax Service.
3. A successful project was initiated, involving the use of the IBM computer to uncover non-filings by running taxpayer listings against telephone company bills.

Tax evasion not only consists of filing false returns, but it also includes those persons who willfully fail to file and to declare income on which tax is payable. The Telephone Company of Santiago has furnished the Service a complete set of approximately 200,000 duplicate IBM punch cards with the name and

address of all phone subscribers in Chile. Phone
subscribers in Chile usually would have a sufficient
income to have to file a tax return. Therefore,
those who appeared as not declaring became excellent
leads for fraud investigations. By use of the IBM
cards and the computer, a rapid and efficient correlation was made. Many civil cases and some criminal
cases resulted from this project.

Other projects were envisioned making use of the
IBM punch cards of other public utilities, such as
the Gas and Electric Companies.

As part of the systematic approach for the development of information concerning criminal violations
of the revenue law, a group identified as the coordination section was started in the Intelligence Division. This group obtains from all available sources
information regarding indicated tax evasion, as well
as identification of suspected tax evaders. The files
of this section include news clippings, government
reports, informants' communications, and other information received about suspected tax evaders.

Training Seminars

As the next step, a seven-week seminar was
started for supervisory personnel. Two and a half
hours each week were devoted to this seminar. The
purposes included:

1. The discussion by supervisory personnel of
    the new manual, containing policies and pro-
    cedures for the Intelligence Division.
2. The discussion and evaluaticn of the work of
    the branches of the Intelligence Division.
3. The training of personnel regarding their
    responsibilities and duties as supervisors.
4. The discussion with supervisors as to means
    of getting results from the men being super-
    vised.

A basic course covering the work of the special
agents was written and presented to all special agents.
For all incumbent agents, the course lasted four months
and consisted of three hours training each week. This
pattern of training is used so as not to generally
interfere with the regular investigatory work of the
agent. Much of the material used in the training
course was condensed and printed in the format of a
handbook, which was given to each staff member.

Field training for inspectors of the Audit Division was also provided. This training involved the technique of detection of fraudulent practices by an inspector while conducting a regular audit of a taxpayer.

The next step, to put the Intelligence Division on an effective operational basis, was now put into effect. This program involved the following:

1. Decentralization of intelligence operations to Regional and Zone levels.
2. Staffing and training of Regional and Zone personnel.

One of the most useful actions during this period was a seminar conducted by the Chief Counsel of the Tax Service for the judges of those courts dealing with tax cases. This was a key factor in turning the attitude of the courts from indifference to these new tax cases to appreciation of the importance of the problem. Also helpful were several meetings held by the Chief of the Fraud Division with the Subsecretary of Justice on the same problem.

Evaluation of Results

In February 1965, the first taxpayer was convicted of tax evasion. This was the first case in the history of Chile and, as far as known, the first case in Latin America.

Over 85 taxpayers have been jailed since then by the Court of First Instance while their cases were being evaluated for the other court. To date there have been six final convictions. In many of the other cases only fines and penalties were imposed because some of the defendents had already been in jail for some time.

The pipeline of cases is full, from a few inactive items, jacketed cases, under legal review and awaiting trial cases. The Department, now with 87 trained and well-led employees, is part of the Tax Service and accepted by the government and people.

The yearly schedule calls for two cases a month to go to the courts and it is generally being met.

Procedures have been installed and are effectively operating for close supervision of investigations for

timely completion; also for surveys to determine tax
evasion areas and identify specific tax evaders.   A
system for reporting all pertinent current data regarding individual cases which will aid supervisors
and management in determining progress and deficien-
cies in the progress of investigations is operating.

A monthly analysis is made of operations and
production and a summary narrative report is prepared
by the planning branch.   This aids supervisors and
and management.

One principal concern of supervisors and managers
in intelligence operations is how to utilize manpower
properly for timely completion of cases of substance.
The function needs a well-balanced program of tax
evasion cases against representative groups in the
professions, businesses and all economic areas.
Therefore, a compilation of evaluation standards and
supervision principles, as applicable to intelligence
operations, has been established by the Chief Intelligence Department.   These procedures and techniques
have been consistently followed.   They are written in
a comprehensive manner so that supervisors and managers
can use these documents as a systematic plan to follow
through on evaluations of operations and effectiveness
of supervision.

The comprehensive survey of all criminal aspects
of the law, as well as procedural rules of justice
that affect intelligence operations, caused a legislative program to be developed which would facilitate
intelligence operations and the prosecution of tax
cases through the courts.   The most important of the
recommendations is one requiring banks and financial
institutions, as well as all persons having knowledge
of a taxpayer's financial affairs, to furnish such data
to the Chilean Tax Service.

CHAPTER **11** PERSONNEL
MOTIVATION

The personnel function in Latin America, or indeed in any part of the world, must be constructed
within the culture, habits, and requirements in each
individual case. The personnel system must aid in
the overall management of the tax service and, most
important, must meet the needs of the employees in
such a way that they will be motivated to the maximum
in terms of production.

Motivation and satisfaction are difficult in that
they both deal with the future. You cannot motivate
a man by giving him what he already has or what he
does not particularly need or want. For example, as
the salary scale becomes progressively better, especially in relationship to what others in their social
group get, the motivation of succeeding salary increases become less and less.

PERSONNEL SYSTEM REQUIREMENTS

A personnel system has to achieve the elemental
bonds which any organization needs to keep functioning
well. These bonds are achieved by:

1. Studying and setting down job tasks and
specifications, and from that job classifications,
salaries, and status. This will assist in developing
collaboration and coordination within the organizational framework set by top management.
2. Systems and methods to ensure motivation of
employees by rewards and penalties and a system of
safety valves to keep discontent at a minimum.
3. The setting up of a status system that will
give each man an identity in the structure in terms
of his power to make decisions. This must be tied in
to the status system of the country.

While all countries have a chain of command,
those from whom you take orders and those to whom you
give orders, it is only in the most advanced countries

that there has developed the horizontal collaboration
necessary to effectively run a large organization.
Horizontal collaboration is the voluntary working
together of supervisors on the same level in terms of
achieving the objectives of the total organization.
This develops only where either the training or the
development of executive personnel has oriented them
to a collective feeling of union with their peers.
Satisfaction is gained from group achievement as well
as from individual achievement. The former is con-
spicuously absent in many countries and is a factor
that has to be developed by training, example, and
other management techniques.

     The problem facing the personnel function, there-
fore, is to convince the personnel of the tax service
to want to comply with the organizational manual or
the job descriptions; to perform adequately despite
an intensely individualistic attitude toward their
work and general lack of interest in the purposes of
the agency for which they work.

     This is not a situation particular to a tax ser-
vice but rather to the culture within which it operates.   Journeymen may keep techniques secret from
their helpers, supervisors may withhold information
from their colleagues or even their superiors in order
to make themselves indispensable. The entire information system becomes defective and it is one of the
major jobs of the tax executive to change this by
various techniques, but more particularly by creating
the "desire" that this attitude be minimized.

     The relationship at the lower levels between
supervisors and subordinates varies somewhat from the
above in that the paternalistic bond is more evident.
Usually the less developed the country, the more common this paternalism is. The relationship between
supervisors and subordinates becomes a very personal
one and the supervisor's responsibility goes beyond
the office boundaries and into the subordinate's
general welfare. In this relationship an evaluation
system, no matter how complicated or how modern, cannot be expected to work since evaluation is based on
personal relationships rather than on the work performed.

     Just to make the personnel job a little more
difficult, most underdeveloped and specifically most
Latin American countries, have systems in both law
and custom that make it from difficult to impossible
to fire a man and, generally speaking, even when a
man has to be transferred because of incapability,

he does not lose his salary and in many cases not even
his rank. This tremendous difficulty in punishing
inadequacy, laziness, and inefficiency makes it just
as difficult to reward effectiveness and competence.

In Chile continuing difficulty, in both the reorganization and the effective operation of the Tax
Service, was caused by the personnel system that,
coupled with administrative custom, had been built up
over the years.

Under this system, there was no relationship
between a man's job and his salary, since every 5
years (by statute) his salary was increased to the
next grade--but not his position. Therefore, if you
asked a man what grade he was he could say grade 4 in
salary and grade 1 in position. There could be a 3-4
grade difference between the salary and grade. Promotion theoretically was based on merit. However,
since over 95 per cent of the entire Service received
the maximum evaluation rating of 120 points, promotion
was based on the next item to be considered, seniority.
The administrative law, plus custom, furnished so much
protection to the job holder that it was very difficult, almost impossible, to punish bad work, while at
the same time making it just as difficult to reward
good work.

As a result, most men worked according to their
conscience. If they had none, their work was minimal.
This system, plus the old tradition of decisions being
made only at the top, resulted in a phenomenal bottleneck operationally, and the peculiarity of supervisors
who at the same time as they requested more staff,
admitted that half of their staff was not working.
The answer usually was to try to give them more staff
because nothing could be done with the staff that was
not working.

None of the other changes could be made operational until this system was discarded and a modern
personnel system, based on job classification, a promotion and salary policy that equates job duties and
responsibilities with pay, an effective rating system,
and other personnel improvements were put into operation.

The Chilean Plan

A comprehensive study of the personnel situation,
including the training of Chilean counterparts in job

classification techniques, was made during one year.
The specific changes which could be made either administratively or by a new law that would change this
system were outlined. The report was finally completed
and copies were distributed to the Director, four
Subdirectors, Department Chiefs, the Head of the Welfare Association, the Head of the Inspectors' Union,
two Regional Directors, and two Zone Administrators.
Discussions were held on an individual basis with
these people in order to clarify sections of the report and in some cases to make amendments and suggestions.

At a meeting of all these individuals, the following steps were agreed upon:

1.   The O&M Department was to start immediately
in drawing up a series of position descriptions for
all key jobs in the Tax Service.
2.   An attempt would be made to get an expert in
the job classification area to work with the O&M
Division in the development of position descriptions.
3.   Meetings would be held at regular intervals.
A follow-up report section by section (making such
changes as necessary) was prepared to present the
comprehensive program and to urge legislation to put
it into effect.
4.   Those changes which could be made administratively would be detailed and put into operation as
soon as possible.

Some progress was made during this time in putting
into effect a better rating system, using the job
classification system developed during 1964, and in
starting the rewrite of the Personnel Manual.

It may be noted that a volunteer group developed
the basic policies of the new personnel system preliminary to the arrival of any of the personnel advisors. It consisted of the Subdirector of Administration, the Chief of the Personnel Department, the
Chief Council of the Service, one Regional Director,
the Presidents of both unions inside the Internal Tax
Service and the advisor. This group worked from 7 to
10, two evenings a week for about five months.

During the entire project, excellent relationships were maintained both with unions and with the
various presidents that were elected. They were of
tremendous assistance not only in the personnel area
but in the entire reorganization of the Service. This

assistance came about because they were included in
the decision-making process.

Effective Personnel Management

The basic proposals for the personnel system are
indicated below; the amplification of these proposals
are in Appendixes F and G. Except for certain legal
changes, the proposals are operational.

1. Normal curve performance rating system.
2. Merit Promotion Plan--promotion of the best
    qualified.
3. Equal pay for equal work.
4. Job Classification System.
5. Jobs are evaluated.
6. Ingrade promotions.
7. Pay scales related to jobs.
8. Supervisor has control over ratings and
    promotions.
9. Supervisor can reward for good or outstanding
    work (rate high-awards-promote).
10. Supervisor can punish for bad work (rate low-
    holdback ingrade or refuse promotion).
11. Supervisor can motivate work-force.
12. Job descriptions with job qualifications
    and work standards.
13. Unit Staffing Standards.
14. Personnel distribution on basis of workload
    and mission.
15. Personnel records and reports to meet needs
    of current Personnel Programs.
16. Training input based on known requirements.
17. Job analysis and position classification.
18. Personnel procedures to operate personnel
    programs to carry out objectives.

As noted previously, the effectiveness of any
tax administration process is in direct relationship
to what a taxpayer <u>thinks</u> a tax service is doing, and
may do, if he does not pay his legal share of the tax
burden. In order to create a climate for conformity,
the specific actions noted previously are of value
only if the taxpaying public knows about them and
makes the appropriate conclusions. Public information,
therefore, is not merely a minor adjunct to a tax
structure but a necessity to the major purposes of an
effective tax system.

OBJECTIVES AND FUNCTIONS

The great majority of employees in a tax administrative system have contact with the public. The way
they conduct themselves is one of the more important
aspects of a public image. The policy guidance, staff
assistance and training necessary for public confidence both in the courtesy and the effectiveness of
the tax system should be guided by the Public Information Department. They should be the technicians in
this field. The functions assigned to this division
should normally include all or part of the following:

1. Keeping the public informed of the day-to-
day filing deadlines, rulings, legislation and other
matters which it needs to know in order to pay taxes
properly and on time.
2. Working with, assisting, and guiding the line
and staff operating divisions to secure the right
publicity at the right time in order to develop the
proper "taxpayer climate."
3. Cooperating with and furnishing materials to
the schools and other areas of public dissemination of
information in order to train future citizens in the
necessity for taxation, the uses of tax revenue, and
their rights and obligations to file an honest tax
return.

4.   In conjunction with the line and staff operations, support and program systems of taxpayer services and assistance both for the filing period and
during the year. This is to create an image of a tax
service that is always willing to help the taxpayer in
every way possible.

The above functions are those which they could
and should be charged with. They are the objectives
around which the daily work and the internal structure
should be organized.

In order to carry out the above functions properly, the Public Information Department must:

1.   Act as a middle man between the technical
areas and the taxpayer. It should utilize all communications media to provide taxpayers with all the information they need to meet their tax obligations with
a minimum of inconvenience.
2.   Review form letters, reception areas, and
other service areas to assist in ensuring that the impact on the public is the one desired by the Tax Service.
3.   Work with the Training Department in developing materials to give all employees a better understanding of the skills involved in sound taxpayer
relations.
4.   Work with architects and the facilities staff
to ensure that signs, design, and layout standards
will make service to the taxpayer well-organized.
5.   Publicize through all news media the usual
errors made in filing tax returns so that the public
will be alerted and will not be disturbed by any
necessity for correction of returns. As part of the
usual dissemination of information to all newspapers,
a series of question-and-answer columns covering those
questions ordinarily asked in district offices, should
be widely distributed.
6.   Initiate, in conjunction with the operating
staff, seminars and meetings for dissemination of tax
information to industry and tax practitioners and provide the fact sheets, reprints of speeches and articles,
films and other background material necessary.
7.   Prepare or supervise the preparation of high-
quality television films and radio programs and arrange
for their programming by the appropriate stations.
8.   Taxpayer assistance, especially before the
filing period, should be the staff responsibility of
the public information function. It should check this
service in terms of possible public reaction.

All the specific items listed above are suggested
methods for the development of the proper public attitude toward the tax service. There are many others
which would have to be tailored to the needs of each
individual country.

Historically, public information service in the
tax area has been, at the best, controlled by news-
papermen. Some of them have a broad enough conception
of their function so that the above approach or part
of this approach was used. At the worst, the function
has been merely a public relations one for whomever
happened to be director of the tax service at the
moment.

It is suggested that the next development in this
area should be the one that has been taken up by most
large advertising firms. The tax service itself has
a product to sell, i.e. the creation of a tax climate
that will result in a minimum of evasion and a maximum
of compliance. To properly do this, some of the knowledge developed in recent years by the social sciences
should be used. The public information function should
have available to it, either on the staff or as advisors, sociologists, psychologists, anthropologists,
and others in the area of these social disciplines.

Staff responsibility for the development of the
proper relationship between the tax service and the
taxpaying public should be centralized. All areas of
public contact must be pointed toward one goal.

A division that will have as much technical knowledge of this specific area as either audit or collection should be created. Their relationships to other
segments of the organization would be the same as any
of the other major staff functions. This division
would develop and program the broad objectives to be
achieved and give leadership to the whole tax service
in achieving each phase toward this ultimate objective.

THE CHILEAN PLAN

In Chile, reorganizing this function was one of
the more difficult areas of change. The purpose was
to secure publicity of all types and by any and all
means concerning the reorganization of the Service,
the new auditing functions, tax fraud, and any other
information that would make the Chilean people "tax"
conscious. To a great extent this was achieved. Were

newspaper clippings measured, they alone would produce
a pile many feet high. Radio and TV coverage has been
extensive. The administrative changes, the law
changes, the property tax evaluation, etc., has for
the first time made taxes a newsworthy item. Tax
courses have been introduced at the high-school level.
Taxpayer assistance and telephone service has been
initiated and is being widely used by the taxpayers.

The "teaching taxes" program has been received
very well by both the tax people and the schools in
Chile, but has not as yet reached the point where it
is operating as well as it should.

The responsibility of the Regional Directors and
Zone Administrators to carry out a well-formed publicity program was finally accepted in every region.
The entire concept of Public Information as one of the
major vehicles in tax assessment and tax collection
has become a part of the daily operation. A tremendous help in this has been the development of course
material for training executives and the supervisory
development material which has been given to all key
staff members.

Before reorganization, the Public Information
Division operated by purchasing space in the newspapers
or radio--like any other advertiser--and by occasion-
ally getting a few lines free. The budget was a very
substantial part of the Chilean Tax Service budget.
The idea that taxes is "news" had not yet been accepted
by the newspaper or radio media and definitely not by
the Tax Service itself. The concept that well-written
publicity about taxes could be published in newspapers
and magazines because of its news interest was not
recognized.

Working with the younger men of the Department,
a good program of visits to newspapers, magazines, and
radio stations was initiated. In addition, the top
staff of the Tax Service started to become public relations conscious and, with the addition of public
relations men at each regional level, the program
started to move. Interestingly enough, when this
happened, the national level accepted the new philoso-
phy and started to move also. They did some excellent
work in advertising the basic tax news releases on
"due dates," types of tax and instructions for filing
taxes. Full credit also must be given to this department in operating and taking the responsibility for a
telephone "taxpayer assistance" system which was

initiated in 1963 and has continued with success since
then.   Full-page newspaper ads were taken by the Service and, with the help of audit technicians, the systems and methods developed for handling taxpayer
questions were very well done.

Despite all this, it was difficult, if not impossible, to develop a fully integrated and operating
department.   An advisor in public relations worked
with the Department for six months, but to little
avail.   An attempt was made to solve the problem
by sending a selected man to the United States for
training, and, on his return, he was attached to
the office of the Director, Chilean Tax Service.
Of great assistance during this time was the backing
of the top staff and their interest and understanding of the importance of a good public information
program.   Many excellent contacts were established
with magazines and newspapers, especially by the
Tax Fraud Department, which always had newsworthy
items.

CHAPTER **13** STATISTICS
AND CONTROL

The purpose of a statistical system is to gather
data so that all levels of the operation of the tax
service know the amount and quality of work being produced. Control is a statistical system that not only
presents quantitative and qualitative data, but by
the development of standards against which to measure
this data, permits acceptable evaluation. In addition,
a "control" always has within the system a feedback of
the pertinent information to the action or correction
point. It should, also, by diffusion of feedback,
permit a review to ensure that the proper action is
actually taken. This is true both of quality and
quantity controls.

The control system usually does not indicate what
action is necessary, it merely points out that within
the program or standards developed to achieve an objective, some point of the operation may be failing.
The action point, therefore, must have the authority,
the resources, and the ability to correct the failure
before it grows.

It is obvious from the above that one cannot
"control" without standards or a predetermined program to "control" against. In order to keep the work
necessary to maintain the system to a minimum, certain
techniques are used.

The usual techniques are:

1. Use of key items only. A key item is some
measuring point in the operation (a form, listing, or
operation) on which other items are interdependent,
i.e. they always bear some consistent relationship to
the key item. By measurement of key items, therefore,
we can measure several others at the same time
2. Frequency distribution. This is usually
graphed to show the number of times an item occurs at
various levels. Its value is in showing the range of
an operation and, therefore, it can be used to set
both quality and quantity standards.

137

3. Sampling inspection. It aids in evaluation of any process which, because of the great volume of items, would consume more time than warranted by the value of the data. A sampling technique could be random sample, spot check, or other acceptable device that will give a valid probability return. This is usually used for the evaluation and setting of standards of quality. In the collection process, this is usually used in the evaluation of IBM card punching, indicating collections of specific types of returns, listings of taxpayers, etc.

There are other techniques used; the above are noted as major examples.

It is well to note that a standard can be determined for any tax operation. Field audit for example, due to the impossibility of determining time on any one case, very frequently is not included. Extending the time interval for control for a 6-month to 1-year period, in order that a sufficient number of cases can be included, will give a very close average per case to use for either administrative or budget purposes.

In setting up a statistical control system, the basic information is always secured from the lowest level of the operation. Since this level is the one in which the work is actually performed, care must be taken to make the burden of reporting as small as possible. To do this, a complete study of possible reporting items must be made and "key" items selected from this that not only are the most important in terms of count and control, but also are in a standard and measurable proportion to other items which, therefore, do not have to be counted or controlled.

The reporting process and report forms must be simple. In general, the more complex the process, the easier to have error and possibly deliberate fraud. A simple system is the most difficult one to deliberately falsify.

For internal control purposes, charts and tables are merely a compilation of the basic statistics into the format necessary to run the organization at each level. For example, the basic statistical production achieved by the Tax Inspector is compiled inspector by inspector by the Group Supervisor of the Audit Group. The Chief of Audit keeps his statistics by groups without bothering with the individuals since his responsibility is for the operation of the groups, not the individuals. The Regional Chief of Audit will keep his statistics by the District Offices, for he again is responsible for the audit operation in the district, and so forth, to the statistics to be compiled for the Director General. This approach to statistical control is valid for all functional areas.

In addition to this internal statistical control, there may be a compilation of various figures necessary in terms of policy decisions or for planning purposes. Since all statistics create a very heavy workload consideration should be given, insofar as possible, to gathering that type of material on a spot-check or irregular basis rather than a monthly reporting.

The basic consideration in setting up the system, therefore, is what information is necessary for the chief of the lowest level of the organization, in the various functional areas, to properly and effectively run the level for which he is responsible.

In Chile, the reorganization of the Internal Tax Service of Chile had provided a structure which could increase the effectiveness of tax administration at every level. It was recognized at the outset, however, that there existed no system of control to ensure that operations would go as planned. The relay of quantitative and qualitative data, especially concerning the functions of processing and auditing tax returns, was lacking.

Working closely with officials of the Chilean Tax Service, a complete statistical reporting and analysis system was designed which the Chilean Tax Service put into effect in the spring of 1964.

The results of this work in the audit area was a development of a simple yet complete control system. (Instructions issued at the inception of the system and the four key forms used are presented in Appendix H. The twelve controls for use by the National Offices are omitted, since they are basically compilations for executive control and use the same data and approach as the first four.)

CHAPTER **14** REAL PROPERTY
TAXATION

Real property taxes, theoretically, should be
the easiest type of tax to collect. Real property
cannot be hidden; the owner, in order to be able to
claim the property, must be registered in some way,
and the collection of the tax, since the property is
always available for the government to take appropriate action, should be even simpler. Unfortunately,
in most countries the people who own real property
are usually among the most powerful politically and
economically. Taxation of real property is frequently
more a political problem than a problem of technique.

REAL PROPERTY TAXATION
SYSTEM REQUIREMENTS

In approaching the taxation of real property,
there are four key points that must be solved administratively: 1) the description and location of the
property; 2) the tax policy including the taxability
of the property; 3) classification; 4) value and
assessment. While each factor must be determined
separately, systems for all of them have to be set up
before a real property assessment and collection system can be made operative.

Description and Location
of Real Property

Obviously, no real property can be taxed until
the government knows exactly where it is and it is
described in terms that lend themselves to classification and assessment. There are two main methods
for identifying land and improvements. (Improvements
usually include the buildings that are on the land.)

One method is by means of specific descriptions
that give the exact boundaries of the land in relationship to a known landmark. The other is by reference to a map devised for that purpose.

A description of property by boundaries tied down
to landmarks is practically always inaccurate, usually
lengthy andk unless the record-keeping system is extremely precise, difficult to locate. In addition,
the maintenance of such description, specifically when
parcels are subdivided or added, is very time-consuming and costly. It is an ancient system which in
this era has outlived its usefulness.

The preferred method of description and location
is by means of a cadastral map. In fact, without an
efficient set of integrated maps, an effective real
property tax is almost impossible. Usually, the map
starts with the country as a whole and gives each political or geographical segment a basic number. This
in turn is broken down by communes or smaller geographical areas. The final number eventually identifies each parcel of property. The numbering system
must be flexible enough to provide for expansion,
parcel splits and parcel combinations.

It is a convenience, especially when maps are
first introduced, to put the house number and street
on urban parcels. Generally speaking, a scale of
1-500 is very satisfactory for urban type properties,
of 1-5,000 up to 10,000 for the larger rural parcels.

While the initial mapping of a country is quite
costly, it is a one-time cost. From that point on,
the problem is the minor one of redrawing or renum-
bering. If aerial photography is available and it
can be used, the accuracy of the maps will improve
tremendously and the cost of the maps will generally
be less.

The maps requirements for a property map system
are not the same as the legal description of the property. What is needed are maps that will show location of property and size of the parcel. Small inac-
curacies, therefore, will not impede the administrative carrying-out of the tax system.

Tax Policy and Taxability
of the Property

The key policy decision in this regard is the
acceptance by the country of the _in rem_ rather than
the _in persona_ concept. In the _in rem_ concept the
property itself is security for the payment of the
tax. With tax rates themselves universally being very
low, this gives the government ample security that the

tax will be paid. With this concept, the problem of
finding the owner, a very major one in many countries,
disappears. Administrative enforcement becomes simple. The collection of the tax, also, in the event
the owner cannot be located, can be accomplished, if
the law is properly written, by collecting from the
renter of the property. He, in turn, is authorized
to deduct this from the rent paid.

If the in persona concept is accepted, the assessment and collection process gets extremely complicated. Many in persona laws permit, for example,
deduction of mortgages from the value. Since mortgages are paid off and created constantly, the administrative burden associated with this one feature
makes the system difficult to administer.

There is a tendency, also, in many countries, to
provide for a large number of exemptions. Normally,
government property and the property of religious
institutions are exempt. From this point, varying by
country, many give exemptions to government employees,
owner-occupied against rented property, new industry,
and many others too detailed to mention. The high
costs of administering these tax exemptions are very
rarely evaluated. The administrative burden of trying
to enforce such complicated systems lowers the level
of the total administration of the tax. The heavy
burden placed upon the nonexempt owner of property
creates a tendency toward evasion. This is especially
true when the exemptions themselves do not seem
basically just and therefore give a moral basis for
evasion by those who are taxed.

Classification

A real property tax usually includes land and
improvements. One of the major problems is to dis-
tinguish between real property specifically, the improvements, and personal property. The line between
them is at times indistinct. Ordinarily, anything
that is tied to a building and is not readily removable
is part of the real property. Those items which are
removable are personal property. An example would be
a central air-conditioning system with its duct work
and other mechanisms tied in to a building (which is
an improvement) compared with a portable room air-
conditioner which is readily removable.

Depending on the government's policy, the tax
law could provide for higher taxes on land and lower

taxes on improvements in order to encourage improvements; or, vacant land, especially agricultural, might
be subject to higher taxation than well-used land in
order to promote economic development.

Value And Assessment

The estimation of the value of a piece of property is generally considered the most technical and
the most difficult part of a real property program.
In general, self-assessment programs, wherever tried,
have been failures. Practically all countries that
have tried them either abandoned them to go to an appraisal program or decided to review the self-assess-
ments with an appraisal program.

Usually one program is developed for the appraisal of buildings and a separate one is developed for
the appraisal of land.

Buildings are usually appraised on the basis of
cost of present replacement less depreciation. The
square-meter costs of buildings are established on
the basis of building characteristics and the code is
related to square-meter costs.

Data is collected in the field on each building,
the data is compared with the code, and the overall
classification or code for each building is determined.
This determines the square-meter costs, and the area
of the building multiplied by the square-meter cost
equals cost of replacement. Depreciation is deducted
and the answer is the value of the building.

The depreciation table is based upon average economic life expectancy. The table is best developed by
means of present worth factors on the basis of a rate
of return that seems to be in accord with local real
estate investment practices. Depreciation is very
difficult to estimate and, for this reason, a table is
essential for consistency purposes. The depreciation
factor reflects the age and condition of the building.
The value of land is usually determined by the use of
sales data and comparisons of sold properties with un-
sold properties within zones.

In an inflationary economy this does not work,
even if the recorded sales figures are accurate. The
appraisal, therefore, may generally require a study
without any preconceived opinions and an estimation
of value based on any data available in the situation.

Consistency of evaluation is in many cases preferable
to accuracy since the tax rate can be either increased
or decreased to compensate. A constant evaluation,
which is fair to all, even those that may run only 50-
60 per cent of value can be compensated for by the
size of the tax rate.

Maintenance of maps, evaluations, assessments and
all other data necessary for a good system is one of
the basic requirements for good administration. A
continuous reappraisal program is much more preferable
to one which is done every four or five years. First,
periodic appraisals have a habit of being postponed.
Secondly, the staff necessary for this type of appraisal must be highly trained and, unless the appraisals
are done constantly, the permanent appraisal staff is
not kept busy while the periodic appraisal staff is
not trained.

The collection and recording of data by means of
either IBM or computer techniques gives modern administrators a tremendous advantage over those of previous years. There is really very little excuse now for
all the data noted above not to be kept accurately, up
to date, and available for use. Systems to do this
can be devised very readily with the use of machinery
now available.

THE CHILEAN EXPERIENCE

During the period between November 1962, and
March 1965, all real property throughout Chile was re-
assessed. This meant individual reappraisal of 957,077
parcels of urban land and 268,521 parcels of agricultural land, a total of 1,225,598 in all.

Before reassessment, total land value in Chile,
as appraised for property taxes, was E°5,775 million;
after reassessment, the new value was E°17,641 million.
Urban property assessments rose an average of 123 per
cent per parcel, and rural assessments rose an average
of 301 per cent per parcel.

The whole reassessment project involved the work
of several hundred men of the Chilean Tax Service
during this period. Two advisors devoted 18 and 24
months, respectively, to the project. The Aerophotogrammetric Project, on whose maps the reassessment
was based, involved over 40 foreign technicians and
several hundred Chilean employees during a four-year

period. The cost of the Aerophotogrammetric Project
alone exceeded $3 million. Project results were used
by several Chilean Government agencies in addition to
the Tax Service.

In 1962, just before reassessment, real estate
in Chile was greatly undervalued for tax purposes.
Estimates of urban areas varied from 10-50 per cent of
market value; rural assessments averaged 15 per cent
of market value. An attempt at general reassessment
in 1956 had failed to bring appraisals up to market
value as of that date, and subsequent inflation had
eroded even the inadequate 1956 base. Rural property
contributed less than 1 per cent of the total Chilean
tax yield, although the agricultural sector generated
over 15 per cent of G.N.P.

A complete revaluation and assessment of property
for tax purposes was ordered throughout Chile by a law
which became effective on November 16, 1962. The reassessment was to take two years and to depend in a
large degree on information furnished by the Aerophotogrammetric Project. This project provided airphoto
maps, a land tenure and cadastral survey, detailed
soil classification, and land use capability studies
for the agricultural sector.

In broad scope the Aerophotogrammetric Project
was an inventory of the national resources of Chile
based to a large extent on airplane photography, airphoto interpretation, and a substantial amount of
ground and laboratory work. The project was performed
by 4 North American companies, under contract, and with
a personnel of 40 North Americans and 200 Chileans. Most
of these men were specialists, geophysicists, carto-
graphers, engineers, photo-interpreters, soil scien-
tists, etc. The project developed and recorded a wide
variety of data which was used in revaluating the
basic farm area of Chile, including the following:

1. Land tenure and cadastral survey.
2. Land use.
3. Detailed soil classification.
4. Land use capability.
5. Measured area in terms of use capability.
6. Type of roads; distance to trading centers.

Accordingly, the project delivered to the Chilean
Tax Service a host of detailed data on each farm directly in line with the provisions of the amended law
of 1962, which requires that all farmlands be appraised

upon the basis of soil classification and in terms of
potential use capacity, with appropriate adjustments
in value for the factors of means of communications,
location and distance.

Under the new law the Tax Service was directed to
use the project material to assess agricultural property according to its best soil use capability; urban
property was to be assessed at market value. As dic-
tated by the law, and for administrative conveniences,
the urban and rural parts of the reassessment program
were organized separately.

Urban reassessment commenced in December 1962.
New personnel were hired for the Appraisors Division.
and an intensive training program began. It was apparent that for efficiency in operation, and to correct
defects in the first six months of appraisals, it
would be necessary to restructure the administration
and personnel of the Real Property Department.

With the newly trained personnel and administration, the main work of reassessment proceeded. Among
the principal steps were the following:

1. A unit value study for land and construction
per province, throughout Chile.
2. Classification of buildings and structures
into 41 types, with detailed descriptions.
3. Development of a property record card.
4. The setting of standards that doubled the
production units per day required of appraisors, and
establishment of methods for ensuring that norms were
followed.
5. Formation of Mixed Commissions to act as
Boards of Equalization in each province.
6. Complete revision of the assessment forms and
records.
7. Development of land depth tables for use in
assessment.
8. Completion of ratio studies in the main
cities.

The entire process took over two and a half years,
from first assessments to final publications of the
new tax rolls. The Tax Service also compiled a field
manual for urban assessors and a more extensive manual
which could be used for training and reference purposes during this time.

In reassessment of rural and agricultural property, comparatively few administrative problems

developed. Reassessment of rural property was partially an extension of the OAS/Chile Aerophotogrammetric Project and used much of the same personnel.
Naturally, project information contributed strongly
to the reassessment program. The Internal Tax Service itself invested over two years and the work of
approximately 250 employees in the agricultural sector
of property reassessment. It would be impossible to
detail the full process involved in reassessment, but
the following actions are indicative:

1. Formation of rural land assessment administrative mechanism; coordination with that of Aerophotogrammetric Project.
2. Appointment and training, when necessary, of
new personnel.
3. Establishment of production norms for clerks
and supporting personnel.
4. Preparation of potential soil use tables;
index of potential use capacity.
5. Preparation of road and distance schedules.
6. Establishment of average provincial land
values.
7. Formation of Provincial Mixed Commissions
(boards of review).
8. Measurement of fields.
9. Decentralization of farm appraisal staff.
10. Development of farm record cards and recor-
dation process.

The final steps for the agricultural reassessment,
as for the urban, were the preparation of tax rolls,
their publication through Presidential decree, and,
most important of all, collection of the tax. Since
in most areas, previous assessments were found to be
completely inadequate, the reassessment had to start
with the base factors.

So that members of the Tax Appraisal Project
would have the benefit of first-hand information of
similar procedures used in the United States, a study
trip was arranged for key members of the staff. This
trip was outlined in detail and suggested tours indicated. Unfortunately, a breakdown in communications
occurred so that the participants spent the major part
of their 3-month tour in Puerto Rico and the opportunity to practice and study procedures used in the
United States was not fully utilized.

Urban Revaluation

Many problems and difficulties were encountered
as the direct result of the late arrival of the Property Tax Consultants, i.e. the field survey which was
to appraise approximately 794,000 parcels had progressed beyond 100,000 parcels. There had been an un-
even distribution of field assessors as the result
of the hurried placement of personnel at the start of
the program. Training of personnel had been limited.

Many meetings and discussions were conducted with
assessment officials to determine the amount and degree of the improvement that could be made in a program that had been in progress for months. An
investigation was made to determine methods used in
all approaches to land construction values. Field
trips were made to determine what methods were being
used to gather field data and what could be done to
improve daily unit production. First inspections revealed a per-man day production of 10 to 14 units. A
ratio study in Santiago Central indicated a spread of
10 to 15 per cent of assessed value to appraised value.
A review of construction classification was made to
determine the scope of coverage in all types of building material and constructions presently in use in
Chile.

When it became necessary to secure vital information early in July 1963, a definite plan for improving existing assessments procedures was formulated.

The plan approved by the Director of the Chilean
Tax Service encompassed the following study programs:

1. Unit value study (land and construction).
2. Field survey of present production and sug-
    gested improvement and control.
3. Urban property record card to be integrated
    with IBM system.
4. Suggested refinement of square-meter land
    depth tables.
5. Basic price schedules or charts (to expedite
    extension of values).
6. Program completion dates for the different
    phases of revaluation.
7. Preparation of a training manual for the land
    assessors.

Following adaptations of the plan, immediate attention was given to improving field procedures and increasing unit production.

Field trips by the consultants were used as a basis to initiate changes in the gathering of field data.

Using the year 1958 as the index base year of 100 per cent, replacement cost index by January 1964 was about 300 per cent.

In a more stable economy, depreciation is one of the most important factors in determining sound value. In a runaway inflation this factor tends to lose its importance.

Classification of the several types of construction presented new problems in determining grade or condition. Depreciation, because of inflation, was given a lesser role in the final analysis of values. Condition of structures remained the major factor in the final determination of values.

Urban land values (tentative) were determined for each section of Chile by the Evaluation Department (Central). Street maps were prepared showing square-meter value for each street. This information furnished a guide for the Mixed Commissions in each province.

Formation of provincial committees had been decreed. For the urban appraisal, 25 Commissions, or one for each province, were activated. Their function was to study tentative values furnished by the Evaluation Department of the Tax Service, and to make adjustments for their areas. Mixed Commissions can be compared to Boards of Equalization found in many sections of the world. Qualifications of the members of the Mixed Commission were specified and include persons of professional status: architects, members of the Chilean Chamber of Construction, and employees of the Chilean Tax Service.

Following the receipt of the observations of the Mixed Commission all information was returned in report form to the Tax Service, then to the Secretary of the Treasury, and finally to the President of Chile. The President, on their advice, determined and fixed the final unit value for all land and construction in Chile.

For many years, vital records containing field
date on eash parcel of urban property were contained
in file folders. Without exception, when efforts were
made to secure information the answer was, "The information you desire is in the field." To prevent this
situation, the first urban property chart to be used
in Chile was designed. It is to be filed in the Zone
Office. Duplicate paper copies for field survey and
commune filing were authorized. From the first draft
in July, 6 months' time was required for final approval
and printing.

A manual for the use of assessors should have been
prepared before the field survey began. Such a manual
was prepared but was finished in midpoint. It was designed to train the new assessors and to furnish additional help for the more experienced assessors.

Early in November 1963, production reports revealed the number of parcels found in excess of the
recorded ones was over 100,000.

Production units per man per day increased from
an average of 12 per day to over 25 per day. Production charts were prepared for each of the 14 tax
zones.

Tentative completion dates were determined. A
weekly report form was established to furnish some
record and control of field production. Zone Administrators were given instructions to mail a weekly
production report to the central offices in Santiago.
In the search for factual information, custom versus
law was encountered many times, i.e. the valuation system was based on the sale price as found in the office
of the recorder of deeds and should have contained
actual sales price, terms, and conditions of a sale.
In actual practice, the buyer and the seller usually
agreed on a sales price for recording purposes by
adding 10 to 20 per cent to the old assessed value.
The use of "recorded sale value" was discarded early
in the revaluation program.

Other sources of information were investigated
to determine current value, such as: property for
sale, advertisements, information from real estate
agents, current replacement cost of labor and material,
construction engineers, and local builders.

The rapid inflation that began early in 1961 made
it most difficult to hold a reproduction cost for more

than 60 days. Constant revisions of cost were necessary. All preliminary planning for the revaluation
program was based on the original estimate of 794,000
parcels of urban property.

There was, however, finally an increased parcel
content of over 163,000 parcels. It became apparent
that the time for total completion of the urban revaluation program would be extended beyond the legal
date.

By March 1, 1964 over 60 per cent of the field
survey had been completed. The many phases remaining
were dependent upon the action of Mixed Commissions.

The following phases remained as of the above
date:

1. Unit values for land and constructions
   (Mixed Commissions).
2. Unit values approved by the Chilean Tax Service, Ministry of Treasury, Presidential
   decree.
3. Extension of unit values.
4. Final ratio study.
5. Manual completion.
6. Preparation and delivery of tax rolls.
7. Application of tax rates.
8. Review and complaints.
9. Preparation of tax statements.

By July 1965, all properties were on the new rolls
and the first payments collected.

Rural Revaluation

Prior to 1956, Chile did not have any good program for the taxation of farm real estate. There was
no dependable listing of farms or their owners, and
vast rural acreages had never been mapped or studied.
A 1956 law required for the first time an appraisal
for taxation of Chile's rural areas. The stated
objective of this law was to appraise rural areas
at approximately 10 times their annual income. Actually, the farm appraisals that were made were approximately twice the annual income. Many farm
owners were missed completely and vast discrepancies
were apparent. The failure of the program was largely
the result of the dependency upon self-appraisal and
assessment by the property owners themselves.

The law of November 16, 1962, decreed a general reappraisal of all real property, specifying the several bases on which the reappraisal was to be done. With respect to farm land, the new law specified that the reappraisal should be based upon scientific soil classification in terms of potential use capacity, with appropriate adjustments for the factors of location and distance. The Director of the Chilean Tax Service ordered that the current revaluation be done in terms of current market values of land, with the taxes to be assessed on 100 per cent of value. The new law fixed the maximum farm land tax rate at 2.55 per cent of appraised value. The individual farm appraising was to be done in terms of provincial average values. Such average values were fixed in consultation with Joint Provincial Commissions of five members, all accredited agricultural engineers.

The advisor on rural land appraisal methods arrived in Chile on April 21, 1963. The first 60 days were more or less concerned with orientation and review of the studies of the rural revaluation project. Field trips were taken to observe in detail the procedures used in tax appraisal. It was learned that much greater progress had been made on urban revaluation than had been made in the rural program. This was accomplished through the assignment of personnel to urban centers rather than rural areas. It was also apparent that the assessors were doing that part of the job which appeared to be easiest, without waiting for the results of the rural survey.

On July 1, a suggested procedure was submitted whereby the entire agricultural land revaluation project could be completed within the legal time limit, that is, November 16, 1964. Administratively this was found inoperable. Therefore, at the end of July 1963, an entirely different approach to the problem was presented. This approach strongly centralized the project for the first year at the National Office and suggested the use of a different group of staff members. It was not until September 10 that approval was secured for this plan. At that time, detailed procedures could be formulated.

Much time spent in October 1963 was in securing field office personnel understanding the essential details of the procedure to be followed in the rural reappraisal program. A beginning was made in the development of formulae for the calculation of indexes of potential use capacity and the land value effect

of the factors of location and distance. Field econo-
mists collected necessary data for early 1964, determined average land values by provinces and by the 12
basic land use classifications outlined on mosaics.

Farm record cards were devised for use in the
project, but a major obstacle developed when there
was an unreasonable delay in getting delivery from
the printer.

In January 1964, it became necessary to establish
a more positive relationship between the staff of the
rural appraisal section and the consultant. Informal
daily conferences were agreed upon so that closer coordination could be secured between the consultant and
the men doing the detail work on rural land revaluation. February 10 was established as a deadline for
detailed replies from the field concerning proposed
schedule of percentage adjustments in rural land
values to reflect type of roads. An agricultural IBM
punch card was designed to meet the needs of the
Chilean Tax Service, under the new law and the contractual obligations of the project. The compilation
of a corrected tax roll by communes was initiated.
This compilation was so constructed that the IBM unit
was able to perform the necessary calculations of
farm values.

Originally the Aerophotogrammetric Project was
supposed to be completed by September 1, 1963. By
March 30, 1964, the project had not yet been completed.
Consequently, all target dates for revaluation and reappraisal had to be changed. The new law required
Mixed Commissions. The objective had been that the
President appoint these Commissions in February so
that meetings could be held in March 1964, which would
result in a Presidential price decree by June 1, 1964.
Originally, the work schedule allowed three months for
this combination of events. Four months would have
been more realistic. In addition, the Commission had
not been appointed on time. This indicated that a
price decree could not be expected before October 1,
1964. Following the Presidential price decree, approximately four months of work was necessary to cal-
culate the farm land values, to appraise the larger
homes, and to prepare the provincial tax roles for
final publication.

APPENDIXES

A

1300

Delegation of Authority. Delegation of Authority,
considered as the action of transferring all or part
of the chief's functions to his subordinates, and
conferring on them the corresponding authority and
responsibility, is not accepted as a general rule by
article 138 of the Administrative Statute. This statute establishes that an employee's function cannot
be delegated, and therefore, it is his duty to carry
them out personally, unless Service laws expressly
authorize such delegation which, in any case, can only
be exercised after the corresponding decree or resolution, as the case may be, has been issued. (The
Organic Statute of the Tax Service permits delegation.)

1301

Faculty to Delegate within the Internal Tax Service. The Organic Statute of the Service and the Tax
Code contain provisions which amply authorize delegation without further limitations than those determined
by the Director himself.

1301.01

National Director's Faculty to Delegate. In
accordance with Article 7 (g) of the Organic Statute,
the Director has the faculty to authorize Subdirectors,
Regional Directors or other officials to resolve certain matters or to make use of some of his attributions, acting "by the Director's orders" in an ample
way, without further limitations than those determined
by the Director himself.

This same faculty is stated in Article 6 of the
Tax Code.

1301.02

Regional Director's Faculty to Delegate. In
accordance with Article 18 of the Organic Statute,
Regional Directors are allowed, according to the rules
issued by the Director, to authorize Zone Administrators or other officials to resolve certain matters or
to make use of some of his attributions, acting "By
the Regional Director's Orders."

The same principle is found in Article 6 (b) No.
7 of the Tax Code, which extends the faculty to delegate even in the case of those subjects which are the
exclusive jurisdiction of this official.

1301.03

Secretary General's Faculty to Delegate. In
accordance with Article 11 No. 5 (d) of the above-
mentioned Organic Statute, the Secretary General of
the Service may delegate to officials of his dependency the faculty to authorize, with his signature,
the powers, documents and proceedings of tax claims
which are resolved or handled within the Dirección
Nacional.

1310

Faculty to Delegate by the Subdirectors, "Visitador General," General Supervisor and Department
Chiefs. The National Director delegates to the officials detailed below, the faculties which are mentioned in each case.

When these officials issue resolutions or sign
documents in fulfillment of delegated functions, the
resolution or document should bear the inscription
"BY THE DIRECTOR'S ORDERS" in capitals before the
signature. In the case of resolutions, the number
and date of the resolution which established such
delegation, should be mentioned in the part corresponding to explanations and considerations.

1311

General Supervisor. The General Supervisor is
authorized to:

    1. Supervise the functional development within
        the different units of the Service; and
    2. Distribute and organize the personnel of the
        Internal Inspection Service.

1312

   Administrative Subdirector. The Administrative
Subdirector is authorized to:

   1. Supervise the functional development within
       the different units of the Service in rela-
       tion to his specific duties;
   2. Distribute and organize the personnel of the
       corresponding Subdirection;
   3. Exercise the attributions contained in item
       (i) of Article 7 or Decree No. 2, 1963, in
       regard to distribution and organization of
       personnel of his dependency, and arrange
       their assignment to any part of the Republic
       according to the needs of the Service, ex-
       cept for 2nd. and 3rd. Category officials;
   4. Authorize or refuse leave with pay of up to
       6 working-days within the calendar year, for
       Dirección Nacional personnel;
   5. Issue the corresponding resolutions to initi-
       ate administrative proceedings, designate the
       investigation and apply the penalties referred
       to in items a, b, c, d, e and f of article
       177 of the Administrative Statute, with the
       same limitation mentioned in point No. 3 of
       this subsection; and
   6. Arrange extraordinary jobs and set their time
       schedule in accordance with Article 50 of the
       Organic Statute of the Service.

1313

   Subdirector of Planning. The Subdirector of
Planning is entitled to:

   1. Supervise the functional development within
       the different units of the Service, in rela-
       tion to his specific duties; and
   2. Distribute and organize the personnel of the
       corresponding Subdirection.

1314

   Legal Subdirector. The Legal Subdirector is entitled to:

   1. Supervise the functional development within
       the different units of the Service in rela-
       tion to his specific duties; and
   2. Distribute and organize the personnel of the
       corresponding Subdirection.

1315

   Subdirector of Operations. The Subdirector of
Operations is entitled to:

   1. Supervise the functional development within
       the different units of the Service in rela-
       tion to his specific duties;
   2. Distribute and organize the personnel of the
       corresponding Subdirection;
   3. Issue instructions on application and audit
       of the taxes, as long as they are not con-
       trary to or change fundamentally the estab-
       lished plans and programs;
   4. Issue rules on procedures to obtain tax data
       and their interchange; and
   5. Resolve inquiries made to him in regard to
       application, term of enforcement or scope of
       tax laws, insofar as the Dirección policy is
       maintained and existing instructions or rules
       are extended or clarified.

1316

   Department Chiefs. Department Chiefs are enti-
tles to give orders to employees of their dependency
on minor changes, with the corresponding Subdirector's
approval.

1316.01

   Chief of Personnel & Welfare Department. The
Chief of Personnel and Welfare Department is entitled
to authorize legal holidays and sick leave for National
Direction personnel.

1316.02

   Chief of Purchasing & Sales Department. The
Chief of the Purchasing and Sales Department is entitled to issue the provisions and regulations related
to the preparation of Purchasing and Sales Invoices
and payment of the corresponding premiums, with a
special numerical order and followed by the letters
"S.B."

1320

   **Delegation of Faculties by Regional Directors
and Rules to be Followed**. The Director, through the
facilities conferred to him by the Tax Code and the

Organic Statute of the Service, delegates some of his
attributions to Regional Directors. In this regard,
Regional Directors should observe the following rules:

     1. Resolutions issued by them should carry the
phrase "BY THE DIRECTOR'S ORDERS" in capitals, before
the signature. It should also be stated that the resolution is issued in accordance with delegation of
faculties, pointing out under "considerations" the
number and date of the resolution which established
such delegation;
     2. As regards monetary matters, Regional Direc-
tors have no limitation and are in any case entitled
to resolve those problems not exceeding an annual vital
salary of the Santiago Department at the date of the
presentation; and
     3. Regional Directors, even in those matters for
which they have been granted attributions, are not entitled to resolve or decide against the National Direction policy established in circulars, resolutions,
reports or the Manual of the Service. If the official
is convinced, from a legal point of view, that the
resolution or decision on a certain matter should be
contrary to the Direction policy, he should abstain
from resolving it and should forward the information
to the Legal Subdirection for consultation. The same
procedure should be observed in those cases where the
Dirección policy has not been stated, or when due to
their nature, appreciation of facts or application of
the law are doubtful.

1321

     Faculty of Representation. The National Director
delegates upon Regional Directors the faculty of repre-
senting the Treasury, whenever necessary, on the application and audit of the taxes the Service is in charge
of within the jurisdiction of the Region. This is
apart from the legal representation exercised by the
President of the National Defense Council.

1322

     Faculty to Grant the Character of Ministros de
Fe. The National Director delegates on Regional Directors the attribution of granting nominally or expressly the character of Ministros de Fe to officials
of the respective jurisdictions or of their dependen-
cies.

1330

<u>Delegation of Faculties of Regional Directors to
Zone Administrators or Other Officials</u>. In accordance
with Article 18 of the Organic Statute of the Service,
Regional Directors shall issue a resolution authorizing the Zone Administrators, other Zone Chiefs and
Local Inspecciones to make use of the attributions
detailed below, also mentioning the rules to be followed by them:

1. Resolutions issued in the exercise of delegated functions should carry the phrase "BY THE RE-
GIONAL DIRECTOR'S ORDERS" in capitals, before the
signature.
2. Regarding monetary matters, Zone Administrators shall resolve cases for amounts which do not ex-
ceed an annual vital salary (the minimum wage) in the
Santiago Department at the date of the presentation.
disregarding the possible retroactive effect of a new
vital salary.
3. The amount shall be established as follows:

(a) For tax claims, the amount of the appealed
taxes (tributas impugnados), disregarding interests,
sanctions, fines or any other legal surcharges.
(b) For informant letters and infractions, the
amount of tax not payed or defrauded is set, according
to what the informant indicates in his report. In
case this information is nonexistent, it shall be the
amount of the fine established by the law and, if
there is a minimum and a maximum, it shall be half of
the maximum.
(c) For remissions (condonations), the total
amount requested at the moment of filing is established.
3. Delegatory officials, even in those matters
for which they are granted attributions, are not entitled to resolve or decide against the National Direction policy established in manuals, circulars,
reports and resolutions. If the official is convinced
from a legal point of view, that the resolution or decision to be arrived at on a certain matter may be contrary to National Direction policy, he shall abstain
from resolving it and forward the information, through
the regular channels, for consultation at the Regional
level.
4. Delegatory officials shall send the Regional
Direction, through the regular channels, 2 copies of
the resolutions they issue, one of which shall be forwarded by the Regional Direction to the Legal Subdirection.

5. The use of the faculties delegated upon Subadministrators or other Zone Chiefs and Inspectors,
will be exercised ordinarily by them, although it is
understood that these faculties are also granted to
the Zone Administrator, who will resolve certain matters when he considers it necessary.

The faculties the Regional Director is entitled to delegate to administrators and other zone
officials, are detailed in the chart that follows.
The level of authority corresponding to the delegated
faculty is marked with an "X."

CHART 1330-1

Faculties to Be Delegated by the Regional Director to Administrators,
Subadministrators and Chiefs of Audits

	Admin- istrator	Subadmin- istrator	Chiefs of Audits Cat.A	Cat.B	Cat.C
I Subjects of a Common Nature					
(A) Resolve requests regarding:					
(1) Refund or credit on account of unduly paid taxes.	X				
(2) Refund or credit on account of fines or unduly paid penal interests.	X				
(3) Condonement of fines applied for delay in filing returns, obligatory reports or inscription requests of any kind, or delay in payment of taxes.	X				
(4) Total or partial condonement of penalties in cases expressly authorized by law.	X				
(5) Claim on statements, drafts, payments or resolutions which may affect the payment of the tax.	X				
(B) Decide on:					
(1) Informant letters received in regard to infringement of tax laws.	X				
(C) Request:					
(1) Coercive measures from the Courts and their renewal in the cases referred to in Title I-- Second Book of the C.T.	X				
(D) Issue:					
(1) Annulment schedules for tax drafts in case of duplication, errors in calculation or "de facto" errors.			X	X	X

| | Admin-istrator | Subadmin-istrator | Chiefs of Audits | | |
			Cat.A	Cat.B	Cat.C
(2) Credit notes, when tax drafts have been made in excess of the amount due, only if annulment is pending and is based on errors in calculation, "de facto" errors, or resolutions.		X	X	X	X
(3) Certificates requested by taxpayers, except those connected with subjects where existing laws establish to keep in reserve.		X	X	X	X
(4) Answers to inquiries by taxpayers of the corresponding jurisdiction on those subjects for which a definite policy has been established by the National Office in manuals, circulars and reports. This source should be indicated when answering the inquiry.		X	X	X	X

II Subjects of a Specific Nature

(A) Income Tax

Resolve requests on:

| | Admin-istrator | Subadmin-istrator | Chiefs of Audits | | |
			Cat.A	Cat.B	Cat.C
(1) Centralizing of any type of accounting, including agricultural, in accordance with the following:					
(a) When the Main Office and Branches are located in Administrations of the same or different Regional Offices, the Administration where the Main Office is located will be in charge of resolving the matter in question.	X				
(b) When the Main Office and Branches are located in different Inspections of the same Zone, the Zone Administration will resolve.	X				
(c) When the Main Office and the Branches are located in the same area of the same Inspection, the Chief of Inspection will resolve.		X	X	X	X
(2) Carry bookkeeping records on loose leaves.		X			
(3) Extension of term for filing Income Tax returns.		X	X	X	X

(continued)

CHART 1330-1 (continued)

	Admin- istrator	Subadmin- istrator	Chiefs of Audits		
			Cat.A	Cat.B	Cat.C
(4) Authorization to perform bookkeeping in only one book or not to carry out bookkeeping.		X	X	X	X
(B) Stamp Tax and Miscellaneous Laws					
Resolve on:					
(1) Requests for payment by monthly income in amounts to be cancelled in valued kind (especies valoradas) in those cases where such system of payment is authorized by law and which should always be delivered at the corresponding Treasury or Treasuries.					
(a) When the taxpayer requests this franchise for various establishments owned by him, which are located in jurisdictional areas of different Zone Administrators of the same or different Regional Offices, the Administration where the Main Office is located will resolve.		X			
(b) When the taxpayer requests to resort to this way of payment for establishments located in different Audits of the same Zone Adminis- tration, the latter will resolve.		X			
(c) When the taxpayer has only one business in the jurisdiction of a Category "A" Audit, the Chief for this Category will resolve, and in other cases, the Subadministrator will resolve.		X	X		
(2) Custom House clearance of products taxed by tax laws on Tobacco, Records, Matches, Lighters and Playing Cards without prior application of seals or stamps. This will be accomplished at the im- porter's storeroom after payment of the tax at the place of receipt.		X	X		

166

	Admin-istrator	Subadmin-istrator	Chiefs of Audits		
			Cat.A	Cat.B	Cat.C
(3) Stamping of invoices, stock certificates and accounting books, when such documents contain notes.		X	X	X	
(4) Exemptions of taxes on shows and money requested from businesses by charity institutions of legal capacity and the Firemen Force, as well as money requested for sports shows, exclusively the physical education type, offered by amateurs.		X	X	X	X
Authorize:					
(1) Conversion of useless invoices.		X	X	X	X
(2) Change of domicile registered on accounting books.		X	X	X	X
(3) Use of the same accounting books in the following cases: (a) Modification of firm name. (b) Dissolution of partnerships in which one of the parties is left in charge of the business.					
(c) Founding of a partnership in which one of the parties furnishes funds for the business.		X	X	X	X
(4) Payment of tax on entertainment through the "bordereax" system, only in case of occasional shows.		X	X	X	X
(5) Exchange of tickets with paid taxes.		X	X	X	X
(6) Exemption from tax on travel abroad for those people of scarce resources who make trips for reasons of sickness or strict necessity, in accordance with **Article 4 (m)** of Decree No. 1.729,1962. They should prove the invoked reason through a certificate issued by the Social Work inspector if founded on scarce resources, or through medical certificate if it is founded on medical reasons; and through written request when strict necessity is					

(continued)

CHART 1330-1 (continued)

	Admin-istrator	Subadmin-istrator	Chiefs of Audits Cat.A	Cat.B	Cat.C
alleged, which will be certified by the delegate official and should be attached to the respective file.	X		X	X	X
Certify:					
(1) The tax corresponding to a document issued abroad for the purpose of legalizing it by the Ministry of Foreign Affairs.		X	X		
(C) Sales Tax (Tax on Purchases and Sales of Personal Corporeal Property)					
Resolve:					
(1) Requests for centralization of the tax return and/or payment of taxes prescribed by the Sales Tax Law:					
(a) For payment of Sales Tax in a Treasury which is not the one that would correspond for payments, but located within the jurisdictional area of the Zone Administration.		X			
(b) For payment of Sales Tax in a Treasury which is not the one that would correspond for payments, but located within the jurisdictional area of the Audit.		X	X	X	X
(2) Tax refunds in those cases where a sale is cancelled due to reconciliation (adjustment, settlement) or for some other cause.	X				
(3) Authorize the use of waybills for delivery of sold goods, with charge to current accounts. The corresponding invoice or bill should be issued afterwards.		X	X		

168

	Administrator	Subadministrator	Chiefs of Audits Cat.A	Cat.B	Cat.C
(4) Destruction of used invoice books, when requested by the taxpayer.		X	X		
(5) Payment of the tax on long-range contracts at the same time as obligations emanating from them are being fulfilled.		X	X		
(6) Requests to file the Sales Tax return in different periods than the calendar month.		X			
(7) Requests on nondelivery of slips.		X	X		
(8) Issuance of sales slips, disregarding the provisions demanded by Article 24 of Law 12.120 or through mechanized media.		X			

(D) Alcohols and Alcoholic Beverages
Resolve:

	Administrator	Subadministrator	Chiefs of Audits Cat.A	Cat.B	Cat.C
(1) Requests of claims on the production index for wine and chicha filed within the legal term.		X			
(2) Claims on collection of taxes on wine production issued because the "Nonproducer" return referred to in Article 40, was not filed on time.		X			
(3) Request exemption on taxes due to reductions in alcohol and liquor distilleries in those cases contemplated by law.		X			
(4) Requests for extensions for replanting of vineyards.		X			
(5) Requests connected with disposal of production surplus.		X			
(6) Requests for authorization to keep grapes lees for forage.		X	X	X	X

(continued)

169

CHART 1330-1 (continued)

	Admin- istrator	Subadmin- istrator	Chiefs of Audits Cat.A	Cat.B	Cat.C
(7) Requests for change of name, inscriptions or other modifications in the vineyard inscription in the tax rolls.		X	X	X	X
(8) Requests for desisting to file returns as "Nonproducer" of wines.		X	X	X	X
(9) Requests by liquor importers to clear from Customs taxed products without application of seals, after paying the tax in the place of storage or receipt. Such operation should be done at the importer's storeroom.		X	X		
(10) Requests on purchase of alcohols and molasses.		X			
(11) Petitions for overdue reception of inscriptions demanded by law.		X	X	X	X

(E) Land Tax on Real Estate
Resolve:

	Assessor* Zone Chief
(1) Modifications on assessment functions except when they derive from errors in classification.	X
(2) Requests for exemption of Land Taxes.	X
(3) Request to include within ("Los roles de avalúo") the real estate rolls parcels which might have been omitted, then making out the corresponding draft for the Land Tax.	X
(4) Assessment on new buildings.	X
(5) Assessment Reductions for demolitions or withdrawal of machinery.	X

* The Chief Assessors of the Assessments and Audits Section, acting on this occasion as Administrators, have the same attributions mentioned under "Zone Assessors."

	Admin-istrator	Assessor* Zone Chief	Chiefs of Audits Cat.A	Cat.B	Cat.C
(6) Assessment reductions on real estate due to decrease of value not attributable to the owner.		X			
(7) Correction of assessments due to errors in calculation.		X			
(8) Subdivisions in assessment functions, making amendments due to change of name, change of owner, street, number, etc.		X			
(9) Reduction of assessment on real property sold at a 20 per cent lower price than the assessment in force.		X			
(10) On special assessments which the law establishes should be carried out by the Service. These assessments do not have any effect on the assessment activities and are for the purpose of setting commercial values, maximum amounts for purchase or reassessment, minimum amounts for sales and compensations. (See Section 8620)		X			
Grant:					
(1) Proportional Assessment certificates for lease revenue in conformity with Law 11,622, and with Article 27 of the Revenue Law, where part or all of the real estate is concerned.		X			
(2) Certificates related with real estate and its assessment, i.e., subdivisions of real estate, sewage systems, Law 9.343, etc.		X			
(3) Total Assessment certificates of real estate, when the Audit assessment roles are completely up-to-date.			X	X	X
(4) Certificate-Article 27 of the Revenue Law when the totality of the real estate is used for business or industry.			X	X	X

* "The Chief Assessors of the Assessments and Audits Section, acting on this occasion as Administrators, have the same attributions mentioned under "Zone Assessors."

(continued)

171

CHART 1330-1 (continued)

	Admin-istrator	Zone Lawyer	Chiefs of Audits Cat.A	Cat.B	Cat.C
(F) Inheritances, Appropriations and Donations					
Report to the Courts:					
(1) Requests for inscription of writ of effective possession.				X	X
(2) Requests to add inventories of assets of a decedent's estate.			X	X	X
(3) Requests to eliminate from the inventories the property which is not part of the inheritance.		X			
(4) Exemption from Inheritance Tax and Gift Tax.		X			
(5) Amount of the tax affecting successions where payment of the tax is delayed, whatever the amount involved may be. This could be done at the Tax Service's initiative or at the taxpayer's request.		X			
Sign:					
(1) Resolutions authorizing or refusing disposal of hereditary property related to successions of taxpayers which failed to pay the Inheritance Tax.		X			
(2) Writs assigning experts for assessment of hereditary property in those cases where such procedure is required.			X	X	X
(3) Writs to fix the date and time to receive preliminary proceedings from witnesses on writs of effective possession.			X	X	X

172

	Admin-istrator	Zone Lawyer	Chiefs of Audits Cat.A	Cat.B	Cat.C
(4) Writs on petition of data for writs of effective possession or insinuation of a donation.			X	X	X
(5) Writs on special handling of writs of effective possession in accordance with procedures established in Article 40 of the Inheritance Law.		X			
(6) All other writs to be presented at the Courts of Justice in relation with Inheritance Tax, Appropriations and Gifts.		X			
(G) Personnel					
(1) Accept or reject applications for leave up to 6 working days per year, requested by personnel.	X				

173

APPENDIX B ADMINISTRATIVE
PUBLICATIONS--
MANUAL SII

1800

Introduction. The object of administrative publications is to communicate to the personnel of the
Service the necessary information and instructions to
carry out their functions.

1810

Responsibilities.

1811

Subdirector of Studies. The administration of
the internal communications system is the responsibility of the Subdirector of Planning and Studies.
This includes setting up the rules related to the
style and format of these publications; their review
before publishing, whenever necessary, to ensure that
the established rules have been followed; to verify
if the necessary coordination and approvals have been
obtained, as well as the necessary contacts for printing and distribution by the units of the Service in
charge of such matters, and finally, to establish and
maintain an adequate distribution formula.

1812

Administrative Subdirector. The printing, distribution and storage of administrative publications
is the responsibility of the Administrative Subdirector.

1813

Subdirectors, Chief of Internal Inspection Department, Department Chiefs. They are responsible
for the initiation and contents of the administrative

174

publications affecting their respective functional
areas and also for updating such publications. This
includes:

(a) The decision on the need to provide a certain
    instruction or information;
(b) That the contents of the publications be
    complete, adequate and in accordance with
    established policies;
(c) That the publications be prepared according
    to the established style and format rules;
(d) Obtaining conciliation and/or approval before
    publication;
(e) Determining and making known the possible
    effect of each instruction.

1813

Subdirectors, Chief of Internal Inspection Department, Department Chiefs. (Continuation) over
prior instructions.

1814

Regional Directors. Regional Directors are responsible for the issuance of their own administrative
publications in the following cases:

(a) To interpret or amplify general policies of
    the Service at the Regional level;
(b) To issue the necessary instructions or infor-
    mation in relation to regional programs; and
(c) To issue the necessary instructions for Re-
    gional Office Administration.

1815

Zone Administrators. Zone Administrators are
responsible for the issuance of administrative publications within the jurisdictional area of the respective zones, in the cases indicated under Subsection
1814.

1840

Internal Tax Service Manual. The Internal Tax
Service Manual is the main media of communication
within the Service in regard to policy, procedures,
instructions and information necessary for the administration and operations of the Service.

The Manual is issued by the National Office and compliance with its instructions is obligatory on all Service officials.

1841

Manual Contents. The Manual is divided into 9 volumes, according to the different subject.

Volume 1 - Administration and General Organization. Describes the organization of the Service, functions of the different units, lines of authority and responsibility, personnel administration, budget administration, administrative services, communications systems for the Service, etc.

Volume 2 - Internal Procedures. Includes all those necessary and obligatory processes performed by the Service in relation to handling and movement of documents.

Volume 3- Audit. Describes the organization of the audit activity within the Service, and provides all the information required by the Inspectors to carry out their functions, except those connected with tax policy itself, mentioned in other volumes.

Volume 4 - Tax Fraud Surveys. This volume includes special procedures established for Tax Fraud surveys.

Volume 5 - General Rules for Taxes.

Volume 6 - Income Tax.

Volume 7 - Sales Tax and Turnover Tax.

Volume 8 - Land and Inheritance Tax.

Volume 9 - Excise Tax on Alcohol and Acts and Contracts.

Volumes 5 to 9 contain tax policy, i.e. information and instructions related to interpretation and application of tax laws, to be audited by the Service.

1843

Format and Numbering of the SII Manual.

1843.01

Manual Format.   (A) The contents of the Manual
will be prepared in loose-leaf folder format, to facilitate handling, when introduction of new pages or
replacement of same when their contents become obsolete, is required.

(B) The material contained in each volume is divided into chapters, sections, subsections and paragraphs, in decreasing order. Each volume will carry
an index at the beginning, where the subjects contained in the respective chapters, sections, subsections and paragraphs will be indicated.

(C) In some cases, to obtain a better understanding of the Manual text, charts are included to
provide a graphic explanation or simply to reproduce
forms used in the Service. Also appendixes will be
used when a specific part of the Manual is amplified
and due to the nature or subject of the explanation
there is no need to include it in the Manual text.

1843.02

Numbering System.   (A) The decimal system is
used to identify the parts of the SII Manual. This
system was developed by Melvin Dewey for use in li-
braries.   The necessary changes have been introduced
to adapt the system to the requirements of this type
of publication. Four digits are used to the left of
a point and two to the right. Each of them represents
a part of the Manual, with the following meaning:

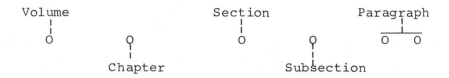

Therefore, No. 6248.21, refers to 6th. Volume, 2nd.
Chapter, 4th. Section, 8th. Subsection, Paragraph 21.
It should be noted that digits placed to the right of
the point will be used as a sole unit, which will
identify paragraphs 01 to 99. In some cases, especially in Volume 3--Audit--paragraphs numbered from
10 to 100 have been used as larger divisions of the
subsections text. Certain numbers have been left

vacant on purpose so that new material can be added
whenever necessary without reorganizing the numbers
assigned to the original text.

(B) Charts will be numbered in accordance to
this same system but taking only the numbers of the
Volume, Chapter and Section where the Chart is mentioned, followed by a hyphen and a number indicating
the location of the Chart; in relation to the other
Charts shown in the same section. This number will
be placed at the heading of same. At the end and to
the right of the Chart, the part of the Manual where
the Chart is located is mentioned as a reference for
an easier identification of the text. The Charts
will go at the end of the corresponding Manual section.

(C) Appendixes will be identified by the number
and title of the volume, the word "Appendix," followed
by a corelative number showing the appendix order in
relation to other appendixes pertaining to the same
volume. E.G.: Volume 6 Income Tax Appendix 1.

1844

   Processing. (A) The department or other organization responsible for keeping up-to-date a certain
part of the Manual, will prepare in draft form the
instructions to be distributed, will determine the
coordination and approval required by the information
and will take the necessary measures to obtain it.
Form No. 1840-1 "Conciliation of SII Manual" (See
Chart No. 1840-1) will be used to this effect.

(B) Once coordination and/or approval has been
obtained, the department of origin will pass these
instructions to the Organization & Methods Department,
using form No. 1840-1 described above, also attaching
copies of Conciliation forms used to obtain approval
and coordination from the other units involved.
These forms, together with the final draft of the
instructions, will be filed by the Organization &
Methods Department as part of the case history. The
Organization & Methods Department will revise the
final draft to ensure it is in accordance with the
established rules and that the adequate approvals
and conciliations have been obtained.

(C) The Organization & Methods Department will
then proceed to prepare the proofs which will be sent
to the Accounting Department for reproduction and
assembly. Printed copies will then be sent to the
General Secretariat Department for distribution.

The mentioned stages should be carried out as
quickly as possible, to provide the personnel with the
advantages offered by this system of communications.

1845

Distribution of SII Manual

1845.01

Objective. It is the objective of the distribution to provide officials, in accordance with a distribution formula, with instructions and information
contained in the Manual in the speediest way possible.

1845.02

Policy. (1) It is the policy of the Service, as
far as distribution of instructions contained in the
Manual is concerned, that they reach the employees that
require them. This means that distribution will reach
up the the last operative level where tasks are performed. Nevertheless, a copy will not necessarily be
distributed to each employee affected by the instruction. Sometimes a copy for each unit will be enough.
At other times, it will be necessary to provide each
employee with a copy. The following factors should
be considered: (a) specialization of the officials
or of the unit; (b) subject of the instruction; (c)
concentration of employees.

(2) Distribution of the Manual will be carried
out in accordance with a distribution formula and by
volume except Volumes 8 and 9, which will be separated
in two because they refer to policies of different
types of taxes. In certain cases it will be necessary
to make a more ample or different distribution from
the one indicated in the formula or a special distribution for certain chapters, sections or subsections
when it affects the work of a specific group of employees.

(3) The Transmittal Guides will be distributed
according to the formula established for the Manual.

1845.03

Responsibilities. The Subdirector of Studies has
the responsibility of establishing and maintaining a
formula for adequate distribution of the Manual (See
1811). The Organization and Methods Department,

through its Manual Section, prepares and maintains an
adequate distribution plan.

The Manual distribution is performed by the General Secretariat Department according to the general
and specific guidelines established by the Organization and Methods Department based on the requirements
of each unit.

1845.04

Distribution Formula of the SII Manual. With the
object of expediting operations, a distribution formula is used (See Chart 1840-2), establishing distribution guidelines by volume and with regard to each
level of the Service.

1845.05

How to operate the Distribution of the Manual.
The distribution will be made directly to Subdirections,
Internal Inspection, Departments, Regional Offices and
units of the Service, in order to achieve a timely
reception of instructions.

Publications will be delivered without letter of
transmittal and with indication of where each copy
should be delivered. When there is a special distribution, it will be marked in the corresponding publication. The units mentioned in this paragraph will
have the responsibility of control of reception, distribution and maintenance of these communications
media. Also, for the success of the system, Supervisors have the great responsibility of ensuring that
the people under their immediate dependency are informed about the instructions they require and which
have been published. A limited number of additional
copies of each issue will be distributed to provide
a small stock in the Regional Offices and Zone Administrations.

1845.06

Guide of Transmittal. (A) The material for the
Manual will be distributed through a Guide of Transmittal. The Guide of Transmittal will be signed by
the National Office Director or his designee authorized
to issue the transmitted instructions. The purpose
of the guide is the following:

(1) Authorize the instructions it transmits.

(2) Bring out the most important features of the instructions thus providing the officials a quick understanding of its importance, to determine if it is necessary or not to give a more detailed attention to the study of the instructions.

(3) Provides instructions so that officials can make the corrections in ink on the Manual. This system will be used when modifications are very small and do not justify the reprint of the page where the change should be made.

(4) Enumerates other administrative documents which have been included in the Manual.

(5) Enumerates and declares obsolete various parts of the Manual, as the instructions are modified, and identifies the pages to be withdrawn.

(6) Establishes the term of enforcement of the instruction, if necessary.

(B)   The Guide of Transmittal carries the date and two numbers. The first of them identifies the volume to which the instruction belongs; the second identifies the number according to the respective sequence. E.G.: Guide No. 8 of Volume 2. These guides should be filed at the beginning of each volume, so that the person who receives it can control the reception of all guides.

(C)   Changes in the text of the volumes of SII Manual will be marked with a straight line at the margin in front of the paragraph where the change appears.

(D)   A list of the Guides that have been issued will be published periodically, and made available to all personnel.

1845.07

Maintenance of the Manual. The volumes are the property of the Service. In each unit, the Supervisor will designate the people responsible for keeping the Manual up-to-date as instructions are published.

Procedure will be as follows:

(1) Receive the Guides of Transmittal;
(2) Verify that they have received all the Guides in a corelative order and with the number of copies that have been assigned to them;

182   TAX ADMINISTRATION

   (3) Proceed to make replacements or include the
        pages which are indicated and/or make ink
        corrections on the Manual; and
   (4) File the guides at the beginning of each
        volume in correlative order.

1850

   Manual Supplements.   (A) They generally contain
similar material to that contained in the Manual itself and temporary instructions issued only by the
National Office.   These will be used in the following
cases:

   (1) When issuance of instructions affects vari-
        ous parts of the Manual and changing each
        part would delay the publishing of instruc-
        tions;
   (2) When the material affects only the National
        Office and Regional Offices or Regional Of-
        fices and its Zones; and
   (3) To issue temporary instructions.

   (B) Identification of Supplements will be made
using the word "Supplement." the number of the volume
to which it is related and a hyphen followed by a
corelative number corresponding to the order of a
specific Supplement in relation to others mentioned
in the same volume.   If the subject of the Supplement
is of interest to the National Office, or Regional
Offices or to the latter and Administrations, the
number should be preceded by the letters DN, R or RZ,
as the case may be.   E.G.:   SUPPLEMENT DN3-1.   The
supplements of the Manual will carry cross-references
relating them with the subject of the Manual to which
they are connected.

   (C) Responsibility for publication of Manual Supplements and the procedures by which they are published are the same as the ones indicated under Section 1810 and Subsection 1844.   The distribution will
follow, in general, the same system used for the Manual, unless circumstances ask for a special distribution.   (See 1845).

   (D) Supplements should be maintained according to
the system indicated in paragraph 1845.07, but they
should be filed at the end of the respective volume.

   (E) A list will be published from time to time,
indicating the Supplements which are still in force.

1860

Circulars. (A) They are publications which contain information of a permanent and provisory nature,
issued by the Regional Offices and the Zone Administrators in the cases mentioned under Subsections 1814
and 1815.

(B) Circulars will be numbered indicating the
volume and the chapter to which they correspond and
a corelative numbering for each chapter, i.e. REGIONAL
CIRCULAR 31-1. In each circular published by a Region it will be indicated if distribution is meant
for Regional Office only or for all the Region. Similar information will be given for Zone Circulars.

(C) It isn't necessary to file circulars in the
Manual, but they should be kept together in the same
place. A copy of the circulars should be sent to
the Organization & Methods Department and to the Department or Departments involved.

1870

Informative Reports. They are administrative
publications which contain information or news. They
are originated at the National, Regional or Zone Office levels.

1870.01

At the National Office level. They are identified
by the words "INFORMATIVE REPORT" followed by the
letters DN, a hyphen, the year and a corelative number. E.G.: INFORMATIVE REPORT DN 63-1. National
Office Informative Reports may be issued by the Director, Subdirectors, Chief of Internal Inspection
and Department Chiefs. They will be distributed by
the General Secretariat Office.

1870.02

At the Regional Offices level. Identification
will follow the same system mentioned above, only
changing the letters DN for R. Regional Informative
Reports should indicate their distribution.

1870.03

At the Zone Administration level. Identification
will be the same as above, changing the letter to Z.
Zone Informative Reports should indicate their distribution.

CHART 1840-1

Conciliation of the Internal
Tax Service Manual

1. TO	3. Date of remittance
2. FROM	4. Devolution term

5. ACTION REQUESTED. The subject stated below is submitted for:

	Signature and Title

Number of part of the Manual	TITLE OF PART OF THE MANUAL OR SUPPLEMENT	Impact on Prior Instructions

6. TO	8. Date of remittance

7. FROM

(Please Mark)	
O.K.	
O.K. with remarks	
Not O.K. with remarks	
Approved with remarks	
Approved	
	Signature & Title

CHART 1840-2

Basic Distribution of SII Manual

Definition of Symbols and Terms.

DN - National Office
R - Regional Office
Z - Zone Administration
I - Audit
D. P. & T. Plant - Managing, Professional and
                   Technical Functions

General Distribution at the National Office, as
follows: 1 copy (except when a different number is
indicated in brackets) for the Director's Office,
Inspection (16), Subdirectors, Departments (2) and
each Section of the Organization and Methods Department, Planning Department and Tax Fraud Department,
Library (2) Telephone Information Service and Training School (the number varies according to the volume).

General Distribution at the Regional Office, as
follows: Regional Director's Office, each Division
and Regional Office Section.

General Distribution in Zone Administration, as
follows: Zone Administrator's Office, each Subadministration and Legal and Zone Office Sections.

Distribution Formula.

Volume 1. Organization and General Administration.

DN - General Distribution.
   - 1 for each Section.
   - Organization & Methods Department.
   - D. P. & T. Plant.
   - Departments of Personnel, Accounting, Training,
     Public Information and Normative Department:
     additional copies of the necessary chapters.

R - General Distribution and 1 extra copy for each
     Division--Administrative Division: additional
     distribution of the necessary chapters.

Z - General Distribution.
   - 1 for each Section.
   - 1 for each Audit Group.

I - 1 for each Inspector.

185

Volume 2.   Internal Procedures.

DN - General Distribution and 1 extra copy for each
     Department of the Subdirection of Operations and
     the General Secretariat Department.
   - Normative Department: D.P. & T. Functions.
   - Organization and Methods: D.P. & T. Functions.
   - Statistical Department: Chapters 2600 and Ap-
     pendixes 1 and 3--D.P. & T. Functions.
   - Resolutions Department: Section 2430 = D.P. & T.
     Functions.

R - General Distribution and 1 extra copy for each
     Division.Processing
   - Processing Division: 1 for each Section.

Z - General Distribution.
   - 1 for each Section of the Subadministration of
     Processing.
   - 1 for each Audit Group.

I - 2 for each Category "A" Audit.
   - 1 for each Category "B" and "C" Audit.

Volume 3.   Audit.

DN - General distribution and one extra volume for
     each Department of the Operations Office (Sub-
     direction).
   - Normative Department: D.P. & T. Functions.

R - General distribution.
   - 1 for each Section of Audit and Processing
     Divisions.

Z - General distribution.
   - 1 for each Section of the Processing Subadminis-
     tration and the Selection Office.
   - 2 for each Audit Group.

I - 1 for each Audit Group.

Volume 4.   Tax Fraud.

DN - Director, Subdirectors, Internal Inspection (16),
     Department Chiefs, Manual Section.
   - Tax Fraud Department: Chief, 2nd. Chief (Sub-
     Jefe), Chief of Sections, Lawyers and Tax In-
     spector.

R - Regional Director and Chiefs of Audit, Processing
     and Legal Divisions.

Z - Zone Administrator; Chief of Zone Audit, Subad-
     ministrator; and Chief of Legal Section.

Volume 5.   General Tax Rules.

DN - General Distribution and 1 extra copy for each
     Legal Subdirection and Public Information Depart-
     ment; Subdirection of Operations; D. P. & T.
     Functions.
   - 2 for each Audit Group.

I - 2 for each "A" Category Audit.
   - 1 for each "B" and "C" Category Audits.

Volume 6.   Income Tax.

DN - General Distribution and 1 extra for each Depart-
     ment of the Operations and Legal "Subdirecciones"
     and the Public Information Department.
   - Income Tax Department: D. P. & T. Functions.

R - General Distribution and 1 extra for the Acts
     and Contracts Section, Assessments, Alcohol,
     Sales and Turnover; Legal Advice, Resolutions and
     Public Information Sections. Income Tax Section:
     D. P. & T. Functions.

Z - General distribution and 1 extra for Acts and
     Contracts, Sales and Turnover, Assessment and
     Alcohol Sections.
   - Income Tax Section: D. P. & T. Functions.
   - 2 for each Audit Group.

I - 2 for each "A" Category Audit.
   - 1 for each "B" and "C" Category Audit.

Volume 7.   Sales and Turnover.

DN - General Distribution and 1 extra for each Depart-
     ment of the "Subdirecciones" of Operations and
     Legal, and for the Public Information Department.
   - Sales Department: D. P. & T Functions.

R - General Distribution and 1 for Income Tax, Acts
     & Contracts, Legal Advice, Resolutions and
     Public Information Sections.
   - Sales and Turnover Sections: D. P. & T. Functions.

Z - General distribution.
   - 1 for Income Tax and Acts & Contracts Sections.
   - Sales and Turnover Sections: D. P. & T. Functions.
   - 2 for each Audit Group.

I   - 2 for each "A" Category Audit.
    - 1 for each "B" and "C" Category Audits.

Volume 8.   Assessments and Inheritances.

DN - General Distribution and 1 extra for the Depart-
      ments of the Subdirecciones of Operations and
      Legal and for Public Information and Machines
      (IBM).
    - Assessment Department: Chapters 8000 to 8600=
      D. P. & T. Plant.
    - Inheritance Subsection: Chapters on Inheritance=
      D. P. & T. Plant.

R   - General Distribution and 1 for Income, Sales and
      Turnover, Public Information, Legal Advice and
      Resolutions Sections.
    - Assessment Section: Chapters 8000 to 8600= D.
      P. & T. Plants.
    - Acts and Contracts Section: Chapters on Inheri-
      tance= D. P. & T. Plants.

Z   - General Distribution and 1 for the Income, Sales
      and Turnover Sections.
    - Assessment Section: Chapters 8000 to 8600= D.
      P. & T. Plant.
    - Acts & Contracts Section: Chapters on Inheri-
      tance= D. P. & T. Plant.
    - 1 for each Audit Group.

I   - 2 for each "A" Category Audit.
    - 1 for each "B" and "C" Category Audits.

Volume 9.   Alcohol--Acts & Contracts.

DN - General Distribution and 1 extra for each Depart-
      ment of the "Subdirección" of Operations and Le-
      gal and the Public Information Department.
    - Alcohol Department: Chapters 9000 to 9900= D.
      P. & T. Function.
    - Acts & Contracts Department: Chapters 9(10)00
      and onwards= D. P. & T. Function.
    - 2 for each Audit Group.

R   - General Distribution and 1 for Income, Sales,
      Turnover, Assessment, Legal Advice, Resolutions
      and Public Information Sections.
    - Alcohol Section: Chapters 9000 to 9900= D. P.
      & T. Functions.
    - Acts & Contracts Section: Chapters 9(10)00 and
      onwards= D. P. & T. Functions.

Z - General Distribution and 1 for Income, Sales and
     Turnover and Assessment Section.
   - Alcohol Section: Chapters 9000 to 9900= D. P.
     & T. Functions.
   - Acts & Contracts Section: Chapters 9(10)00 and
     onwards= D. P. & T. Functions.
   - 2 for each Audit Group.

I - 2 for each "A" Category Audit.
   - 1 for each "B" and "C" Category Audits.

APPENDIX C CHILEAN-AMERICAN
PHILOSOPHICAL
SOCIETY: TOPICS
COVERED

1. The Job of the Supervisor.
2. Concepts of Line and Staff Organization.
3. Job Classification.
4. Delegation of Authority.
5. Communications within the Structure.
6. Human Relations.
7. Office Layout and Machine Use.
8. Statistics and Control.
9. Office File and Document Control.
10. Problem Solving.
11. How to Conduct a Meeting.
12. Performance Standards.
13. Evaluating Personnel.
14. Evaluating Results
15. Process Charting and Use.
16. Planning.
17. Performance Budgeting.
18. The Job of the Zone Administrator.
19. Contents of Functional Statements.
20. Theory of Tax Administration.
21. Public Relations as Part of Tax Administration.

APPENDIX TRAINING DEPARTMENT:
TRAINING COURSES AND
MATERIALS

No. 1 Training Course for Instructors.

No. 2 Fundamentals of Supervision.

No. 3 Course for Group Chiefs (Audit).

No. 4 Vacant.

No. 5 Course for Special Agents.

Course for Inspectors (2nd. Phase).

Subjects:

Auditing	Income
Sales	Sales of Services
Accounting	Inheritance

No. 6 Course for Inspectors (Canvassing and Office Inspectors).

Subjects:

Auditing	Sales Services
Tax Code	Legal Rights
Sales	Administrative Statute
Accounting	Excise Taxes
Income	Inheritance
Alcohols	Organization & Methods
Evaluations	Public Relations

No. 7 Course for Inspectors (Field Inspectors).

Course for Assessors
Rational Administration and Supervisor's Role
Real Estate (Evaluation)
Course for Chief Inspectors
Organization and Methods
Training Course for Office Auditors
Course for Technical Helpers
Information Bulletin No. 1 - Central Library

ORGANIZATIONAL CHART OF THE TRAINING DEPARTMENT

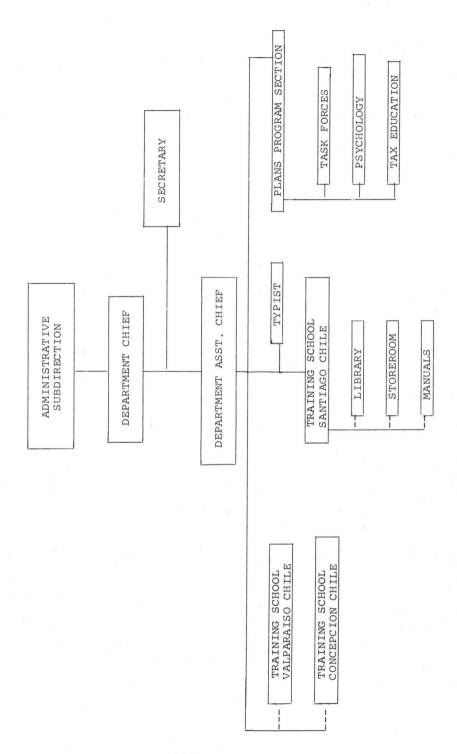

APPENDIX E BASIC PLAN FOR THE
IMPROVEMENT OF
COLLECTION OF
DELINQUENT TAXES

CONTENTS

IV. How the Reorganization should be Effected.

    A. Laws Needed.
       1. Organization
       2. Procedure
    B. Merger between Treasury and Collection
       1. Administrative
       2. Local Offices
       3. Zonal Legal Staff
    C. Effecting the Transition
       1-7.
    D. Operations Pending Law Changes
       1-11.
    Appendix A Chart of Present Organization of Collection
    Appendix B Chart of Proposed Organization of Collection

A copy of the new Collection Law follows:

CHAMBER OF DEPUTIES
CHILE

Article 151: The President of Chile is empowered hereunder to proceed, progressively or at once, within a maximum period of....., with the incorporation of the Legal Collections Department of the Council for Defense of State Interests to the Treasury Department, being able to set new dependence standards, to change denominations and to modify the organization of both entities in such a way as to obtain an effective merger, and to modify the regulations directing the judicial collection of tax obligations in money, being also authorized to change the current judicial procedures into administrative ones including the levy and sale of property. In either case, the intervention of the Court of Justice shall be requested on what regards to the hearing and decision, on first appeal, of exceptions and defenses filed by the taxpayers. Ordinary Justice shall also decree the imprisonment of delinquent taxpayers when it is necessary.

Using this power the President of the Republic shall also be able to grant these services charged with the collection of taxes the same attributes that the Tax Code grants to the Internal Revenue Service and which deal with the inquiry of the assets and properties held by the taxpayer and with the verification of the accuracy of statements requested from taxpayers with the sole purpose of determining ownership of property over which tax obligations may be

collected, and likewise, to empower the organization
charged with the collection of these tax liabilities
to apply pecuniary sanctions that Art. 97 of the Tax
Code provides for the Internal Revenue Service; to
modify the terms for the preparing of the lists of
delinquent taxpayers, uncollectable minimums, and the
terms for prescription of the State action against
delinquent taxpayers as provided by the aforementioned
code; to authorize the compensation between liabilities
of delinquent taxpayers and the credits that they may
have against the State; to establish the power to levy
remunerations of amounts over five minimum vital salaries, and to regulate on the employer's a duty obli-
gation to withhold and make him responsible for the
payment of said liabilities; to reestablish the privi-
lege and preference that the Code of Civil Procedure
provides for State and Municipality credits; to establish the readjustability of delinquent accounts;
to set fines for delinquent taxpayers and to collect
from them the costs of collection; to replace the
present system of fees for Collection Agents of the
Legal Collections Department by a fixed remuneration
in accordance with the scale of remunerations of the
List which is to be made of the Collection Agents in
the new plant which is referred to in Art. 74, no
matter what is the job to which he is assigned, this
cannot mean a reduction of the salaries in force at
the moment when the List is made, established in accordance with DFL No. 1, of 1963, modified by Article
1 of the Law No. 16.010. The Collection Agents who
have been listed in a grade or category inferior to
the one which should correspond to them according to
this assimilation, will receive the difference through
a supplementary payroll.

     Article 152: The President of the Republic is
authorized hereunder to set, separately, the staffing
patterns of the Legal Collections Department and
those of the Council for Defense of State Interests,
and to incorporate afterwards the staff patterns of
the Legal Collections Department to those of the
Treasury Department. The use of this power, that
shall be exercised during the term mentioned in the
above article, shall not mean in any case, the ending
of functions of personnel currently in service, nor
shall it represent a diminishing or suppression of jobs
presently considered in the staff of the Council for
Defense of State Interests, shall not represent a
diminishing in the remunerations enjoyed by personnel
nor the altering of the present domicile of same. The
setting of staff patterns provided in this article
shall not cause the loss of rights enjoyed by the
aforementioned personnel and provided in Articles 59

shall not cause the loss of rights enjoyed by the aforementioned personnel and provided in Articles 59 and 60 of Decree having force of Law No. 338, 1960, nor their right to retire in conformity to Art. 132 of the same legal text, always that on the date of its enactment it would comply with the requisites that said article pursues.

Article 153:   Meanwhile the incorporation referred to in Article 151 above comes into effect, the Legal Collections Department of the Council of Defense of State Interests shall go directly under the Treasurer General.   From this moment on the Treasurer General shall have all the authority and duties that DFL No. 1, 1963, the Tax Code or other special laws had given to the President of the Council for Defense of State Interests, or to the Council itself, on what regards the Legal Collections Department and its functioning. The Treasurer General shall also have the attributions and carry out the duties in regards to the Legal Collections Department and when applicable, that the Organic Statute of the Treasury Department assigns to him in Articles 5 and 16.

The rating of personnel of the Legal Collections Department for the 1967 period shall be affected by the Rating Board of the Treasury in accordance with the regulation of said Service.

Article 154:   Rating of personnel of the Legal Collections Department for 1966 shall be carried out by the Council for Defense of State Interests in accordance to the standards established in its Organic Statute and in its Administrative Statute.

Article 155:   The following modifications are introduced to Art. 22 (letter g) of DFL No. 5 of 1963: a) in the first clause number "30" is replaced by "80," and b) the second clause is replaced by the following: "Within the following 90 days of the respective expiration, will likewise send a payroll of the delinquent taxpayers or contributions not subject to a roll or drawn out of roll."

Article 156:   The Services included in Articles 1 and 11 of this Act are hereunder authorized to effect transfers between the items of remunerations during the first six months of 1967 with the purpose of helping the financing that represents the application of the aforementioned articles.

APPENDIX F PROPOSALS FOR
IMPROVEMENT OF
PERSONNEL
MANAGEMENT

PART I--INTRODUCTION

The proposals contained in Part III were developed
by an advisory group within the Chilean Tax Service,
consisting of high officials of the Service from within the National Office, and representatives of the two
employee organizations.

Virtually all the proposals were agreed to unani-
mously. (In the case of the proposal on performance
evaluation, and on the procedure for promotion, one
of the employee group representatives had some reser-
vations.) At a final meeting of the group, a compilation of the decisions reached, taken from the minutes
of the meetings, was read and agreed to once more, as
the consensus of the group. The minutes of the meetings, and papers presented to the group, contain further details and suggested implementing procedures
for the modifications in existing practices agreed to
by the group. However, these should not be considered
as binding, and are not essential to consideration of
the principles agreed to by the group, for changes in
the present personnel management system of the Service.

PART II--PROPOSALS BY CATEGORY OR
ASPECT OF PERSONNEL MANAGEMENT

The proposals below include, first, the principle
or proposal for each of the listed aspects of personnel management. There follows, in parentheses, ex-
planatory comments or details of suggested implementation, when appropriate. However, only the principle
should be considered as the official recommendation
of the advisory group which formulated them. The
statements in parentheses are not an essential part
of the proposal, but are merely submitted for a better
understanding of the prior statements, or as suggestions for how to apply them.

198

1. Performance Ratings

In order to make more useful distinctions for personnel and internal management purposes in the performance level for the various employees of the Service,
ratings should be made and employees ranked in accordance with distribution on the normal curve. Each
year, management should determine the cutting points
and groupings in terms of percentages based on judgement, knowledge of the employees and supervisors, and
the previous year's experience. There should be no
necessary conclusion that any or all the individuals
in the bottom group are unsatisfactory. An appropriate committee, however, should review the facts about
the performance of the individuals in the bottom
group, independently of the immediate superior's rating.
The committee should determine in each case whether
the employee's performance was acceptable or unsatisfactory, and could also make such additional findings
and recommendations as they believed proper.

(Comment: It is not practicable to have a committee develop facts to review the supervisor's rating
for all employees. However, with the small percentage
of employees--no more than 10 per cent, and probably
less--expected to be in the bottom group, it becomes
practicable to have an independent check to identify
the unsatisfactory employees. A procedure, illustra-
tive of how the principle would work, has been developed. Essentially, it provides for first-line immediate supervisors, with less than 20 employees, ranking
their employees by the quality of their performance.
The supervisors of the superior levels are then responsible for reviewing these ratings, and based on
their own personal knowledge and their opinion of the
quality of the various units under them, making the
necessary groupings.

The groupings might be three, four, or five, and
the percentages might vary from year to year, in accordance with the instructions for the rating in a
particular year. To illustrate, it was suggested that
for the first year there be five levels, corresponding
to the top 10 per cent, "Very Superior"; next 15 per
cent, "Above Average"; middle 50 per cent, "Average";
next 15 per cent, "Somewhat Below Average"; bottom 10
per cent, "Marginal" or "Well Below Average."

With the adoption of a position classification
system, and information available as to the usual grade
level for the tasks which an employee is performing,

this should also be considered in the performance
rating. After a period during which an employee,
doing work below his proper grade level, can be reas-
signed or given the necessary training and opportunity
to do the usual work for his grade--as normally required by Article 35 of the present Administrative
Statute--he may be found to be unable or unwilling to
do the proper work of his grade. In such an event,
it does not appear just to give him a top performance
rating, no matter how well he performs the work of
a lower level than what is typical for his grade.
Conversely, an employee who performs the work of a
higher grade than his own even with average success,
is above average in performance for employees of his
official grade. The adoptions of such considerations
in performance rating would also serve to simplify
the administrative mechanism for promotions and permit more reliance on ratings in the promotion process
than is the case at present.)

2. Promotions

Evaluation by a committee should be used in selection for supervisory and higher jobs, to make recommendations to the appointing authority. In promotions
to nonsupervisory positions eligible employees should
be considered by rating groups (as covered in the previous recommendation), and by seniority within the
rating group.

3. Pay Administration and Position Classification

The pay scale should be linked to the level of the
duties. The structure should be rearranged, with
vertical grades based on differences in level of work
performed, and horizontal within-grade steps, based
on seniority. Recommendations for the proper number
of grades to reflect real differences in qualifications and responsibility, should be made after a preliminary survey of the Chilean Tax Service positions,
and probably should be fixed at 15 grades, exclusive
of the Director instead of the former 25. (Note:
Based on this preliminary survey, it now appears that
15 grades would be the suitable number.)

The horizontal structure should consist of 5 steps,
advancement from one step to the next being based on
3 years' service in the grade. (However, if the employee's service is evaluated as unsatisfactory in a
particular year, after he is rated in the bottom group
on the normal curve, and an independent review

committee confirms that he is unsatisfactory, on an
absolute basis, then that year's service does not
count towards the seniority increase.)

Promotions in vertical grade start a new 3-year
period. The employee is promoted to the minimum step
of the new grade, provided that is at least one step
above his former salary in the grade from which he is
promoted. If it is not, he is promoted to the step
which will give him one full step increase.

Employees are not to lose salary in the initial
classification based on duties actually performed.
However, if because of such a saved salary, the employee is above the normal fifth salary step for his
grade, he shall not upon promotion receive an increase
in pay above the fifth step of the new grade. He may
retain the saved salary if that is higher than the
fifth step of the new grade.

4. Salary Rates and their Adjustments

The rates should be adjusted annually by proportionate changes which maintain the internal relationships of the pay structure. Upward adjustments could
be based on (a) the same percentage that the year's
tax collections have increased over the previous year
or (b) any general pay increase granted to all public
employees, whichever of (a) or (b) is the greater.

(Comments: The principle of maintaining the internal relationships of the pay structure, and increasing it for salary adjustments for cost-of-living
changes is the same as the government system. However,
the alternative method (a) of figuring the increase,
by the amount that tax collections have increased
over the previous year, is different, and is, of
course, peculiar to the Chilean Tax Service. While
tax collections generally could be expected to vary
more or less in proportion to changes in the cost of
living, the proposal above gives an additional incentive to the staff of the Chilean Tax Service for more
effective tax administration. If they bring substantially more money into the government Treasury, this
will have the effect of a bonus for that year in their
pay. The principle is not unlike that currently applicable to some employees of Legal Collections, who
receive a commission on the amount of delinquent past-
due taxes which are collected through their efforts.

The pay structure should be a logical, well-organized one. Thus, if a 15-grade structure of five
increment steps is established, as proposed for the
positions below the Director (i.e. the 2nd. category
of the Planta Directiva, and below) then a logical
structure could be constructed on the basis of the
first step on each vertical grade being 15 per cent
above the first step of the grade below. Each horizontal grade (of five seniority steps) could be a
range of 30 per cent, with each successive step increasing by 7.5 per cent of the first step in the
grade. A table has been constructed and is annexed
showing these relationships, in terms of 1.00 for the
first step of the lowest grade, 1.30 for the top step
of that grade, 1.15 for the first step of the next to
the lowest grade, etc. In 1965 terms, this index
figure would be multiplied by approximately 200 to
give the monthly salary in escudos. The following
year, this base figure might be multiplied by 250, to
effect an adjustment of the desired magnitude. The
table roughly corresponds to the relationships and
spreads of the present grade structure, but eliminates
the illogical aspects, such as the unusually wide
spread in the 5th category, Administrativa Structure;
the almost meaningless salary differences in the
lower grades and the unusually wide ranges in the
higher grades of the executive structure.)

5. Leave

Sick leave should be subject to limitations. It
should be earned at the rate of 15 days per year,
cumulative. However, the Zone Administrator (or official of equivalent rank), should be authorized to
advance up to an additional 15 days per year, in his
discretion; and the Regional Director (or equivalent
official in the Service) should be authorized to advance up to an additional 30 days per year. Such
advances are to be deducted from leave earned later.
The pay for the period of any unearned, advance leave
should be deducted from the employee's retirement.

The use of sick leave within these standards
should not reflect on the employee's performance
ratings nor should the use of leave (paid or unpaid)
for maternity leave.

(Comments: No recommendations for changes are
being made with regard to the present annual leave
system.)

6. Hours of Duty

Professional, technical, administrative and
clerical employees should all work the same hours,
based on an eight-hour day, devoted entirely to official duties.

Abuses of the regular time schedule (e.g. late
arrival, by more than 15 minutes) should be penalized.
Time should be made up, for minor infractions. Salary
should be docked, for lateness beyond a margin of
tolerance, in accordance with a set tabulation previously decided upon by the Service. Visitadores should
check on practices in this regard, to insure conformity.

No specific recommendation has been made in regard to "Elimination of overtime schedules as a method
of Augmenting Salaries" for the Service. In the future, adjustment in salary rates should be made annually. Moreover, the position classification system
should reduce present inequities of pay in individual
positions now compensated below their true level.
(e.g. multilith operators, paid as porters, despite
their special training and more skilled duties). When
this occurs, the problem of possible abuse of overtime
should disappear.

7. Awards

The Director of the Tax Service should be authorized to make up to forty special cash awards to outstanding employees in accordance with pre-established
standards. Selection for these awards should be made
by a committee designated by the Director.

(Comments: This accords with practices in various countries and other jurisdictions, and in private
industry. Such awards have been found to stimulate
and motivate employees to make additional contributions, and the example of recognition to outstanding
employees has been useful to raise the level of accomplishment of the others.

It is common to grant such awards for three types
of outstanding services:

(1) For sustained superior performance, in quality and quantity.
(2) For proposals, which have been reviewed and
adopted, to reduce costs of administration, and improve operations.

(3) For special acts and services which merit recognition by such an award. (For example, outstanding investigations and audits; unusual devotion to duty, including extended hours, in cases of absence of other employees, or in emergencies; temporary filling of higher positions, in a successful and efficient manner.)

A usual limit for the awards for sustained superior performance, is the amount equal to a seniority increment in the pay scale. If the recommendation for a logically constructed pay structure outlined above were accepted, this limit in the cash award would then be 7.5 per cent of the employee's annual salary.)

8. Transportation

Automobiles used by employees for official duty should be compensated for at mileage rates which are fully compensatory, including depreciation. This will require separate scales for urban and rural driving.

Arrangements should be made for the State Bank to loan money to employees, to finance purchase of private cars to be used on official duty, on a mileage basis. Customs duties should be remitted for such cars, but the duty should be repayable if the car is sold, or the employee leaves the Service, within five years.

(Comment: The present reimbursement covers only gasoline and oil, which is inadequate for the true costs. In addition to different rates for urban and rural driving, in parts of the country where driving conditions are very bad (e.g. the desert and the mountains), there may need to be a special "bad conditions" rate, to comply with the principle of full reimbursement of costs, in conditions of unusual "wear and tear."

The remission of customs duties, repayable unless the conditions of official use are met for five years, parallels what is in effect for automobiles destined for use as public taxis.)

9. Discipline and Employee Integrity

The bank accounts of all staff members should be open to inspection by authorized representatives of the Service. A staff of inspectors (ten recommended

at present) should be assigned to the Department of
Personnel and Welfare, to check these bank accounts
and accompanying financial statements submitted by
employees, and to investigate sumarios, etc.

(Comment: Actual cases arising in which tax
fraud or corruption by employees is suspected, might
more appropriately be investigated by tax fraud in-
vestigators from the intelligence activity, who are
more suitable for such activity because of their
special experience and training.)

10. Retirement

The size of retirement benefits should be reduced, on the following basis:

a. New employees (those first appointed after
enactment of this provision) should upon retirement
receive 75 per cent of their average salary for the
last three years of their employment.
b. Old employees (those already on the rolls)
should have the option either of the method under (a)
or the present system. In the latter case their retirement should be calculated on the regular government salary basis, without the benefit of the special
pay rates resulting from annual adjustments under 4
above.

(Comment: Retirement at full pay is unusual in
public administration practice, particularly without
an age deduction for those below an advanced age.
However, because a contractual relationship may be
considered to exist for those already in service,
their benefits should not be reduced without their
consent. However, within a few years, because of the
probable operation of annual increases in the pay
rates, it is likely that the old employees will find
it beneficial to elect option (a) above, rather than
(b). Hence all employees will then be on the same
basis, with retirement at 75 per cent of the rates
then in effect.)

11. Recruitment and Selection

No special recommendations were made on this
subject. In the discussions of the uses of position
classification, however, it was recognized that one
of the advantages of the study of duties performed is
to permit revision of nonrealistic qualifications
requirements (those not matching the duties or the

qualifications actually possessed by successful per-
formers of the work). Better and more realistic
qualification requirements would permit improvement
or recruitment.

In practice, this principle is already in effect
(more or less), for positions in the Tax Service. The
requirements for efficiency and a high degree of competence in the administration of the tax system result
from the need for collecting adequate revenues in order
to support the government's programs. Hence the situation requires objective selection and the recruitment
of properly qualified people. The section on "promotion," (2) above, is an example of use of merit measures in selection: the panel to assess qualifications,
in the case of supervisory positions, and the use of
meaningful performance ratings, for the nonsupervisory.
With more adequate study of the jobs and the perfection
of suitable qualification standards and measures such
as tests for applying these standards, there should be
considerable further improvement in recruitment and
selection.

12. Training

No special recommendations are being made on
training. However, the discussions of the uses of
position classification included recognition that the
usefulness of training can be improved by better knowledge of the duties of the various jobs, and follow-up
of people trained to see that their training is utilized.

PART III--PRACTICAL PRELIMINARY
STEPS AND SUGGESTIONS FOR
COMPLETE EFFECTUATION

A number of steps were taken by the management
of the Chilean Tax Service both to achieve some of
the objectives and administrative improvements covered
in Part II, within the scope of the present laws, and
also to prepare for enactment of additional laws which
may be required before the desirable effects can be
fully realized. Some of these steps have already been
initiated; others should be taken, as indicated below,
in advance of new legislation; and complete effectuation must await a change in law, particularly for a
system specifically relating duties performed to
salaries.

1.   Position Classification - Survey and Related
Preliminary Steps

A survey covering the 3,500 positions in the
Chilean Tax Service was initiated by means of specially
designed forms showing tasks and percentages of time;
which tasks are of primary importance; the supervisor's
opinion of this level of difficulty, for tasks of the
same kind at that locality; and training taken, experience, and other identifying information. By use
of these forms, a complete inventory of positions, by
title and grade level, has been made available.

The inventory of positions was compared with the
existing title, grade, training and other qualifications of each incumbent employee. A variety of management benefits derived from this information, including
of course, as a primary possibility the reassignment
of employees whose official grade and title vary substantially from the grade and title appropriate to the
work they are performing.

After a reasonable period following communication
of the results of this survey through supervisory channels, there should be a follow-up survey. (e.g. about
September-October of 1965). This will serve to determine whether qualifications and rank have been brought
into better alignment with the level of the position.
It is suggested that new descriptions or forms be prepared only where changes have been taking place since
the survey initiated in December 1964; where the positions are unchanged, it should merely be necessary
to state that this is the case.

Employees who are thus discovered still to be
performing work substantially different from the level
appropriate to their grade and salary, should have the
circumstances of each case considered in the subsequent
performance rating period (December, 1965). Employees
unable or unwilling to perform work of a higher level
such as is appropriate for their personal rank, and
who have been given an opportunity to perform such
work, should not receive a high performance rating
for the performance of low-level duties (no matter how
well they perform them.) Conversely, they should get
recognition in the rating, with a high rating, for
satisfactory performance of work usually associated
with a higher grade.

Various other management improvements can be
expected as a result of the information obtained in

the position classification survey. Examples referred
to under other headings include revision of qualification requirements; better selection for training, more
appropriate training course content, and better placement of training course graduates; improvement of
utilization of employees and of work practices; better
information for staffing practices and the budget, etc.

2.   Suggestions for Complete Effectuation

Some legislation undoubtedly will be required
before the Service can accomplish all the recommendations for personnel management improvement contained
in Part II.   It is true that much can be accomplished
under the existing laws, some of which are good but
have not been adequately administered.   For example,
the instructions for performance rating are often
disregarded because each supervisor fears to penalize
his own men, by comparison with those rated by other
supervisors who rate with more leniency.   This per-
petuates a system of meaningless ratings, with most
employees receiving the maximum.   Rating on the normal
curve, to force ranking distinctions among those rated
is essential to stop the present practices.   Also job
information and classification of positions is necessary, to develop meaningful standards of performance
for employees of various grades assigned to work of
different levels.

The present Administrative Statute, in Articles
3 and 35, provides the framework for a classification
system, provided there were implementing machinery for
these articles.   Under them, positions should be classified in level by functions assigned, and employees
should be assigned only to work a job typical of the
grade to which they have been appointed.

With no standards for classifying jobs, and no
systematic information available about the level of
duties actually performed by each person, it has been
impossible thus far to enforce these well-intentioned
articles of the Administrative Statute.

Statements have been developed showing the plan
for a new grade and pay structure (more logical than
the present structure) and for the necessary transition measures.   These are annexed.

With the passage of new legislation, there should
be a more thorough-going job survey than those in
December, 1964, and the follow-up later in 1965.   This

is because, for the first time, an employee's salary
will depend on the decisions made. Provisions should
be made for a greater degree of employee participation
in fact-finding, and the right of appeal. (In the
preliminary surveys, since the purpose was to effect
only management actions such as reassignments and
provision of training, the primary responsibility was
placed on supervisors and management to report the
facts, and the employee merely participated in a
discussion of them with his supervisor.)

Following this survey in depth, from a larger
number of somewhat individualized descriptions, a
smaller number of standardized descriptions can be
prepared and issued, with the aim of covering virtually all the positions in the regions and zones, and
the more common positions in the Nacional Office.
Instructions should be issued providing that the descriptions should be followed as requirements binding
on the employee, unless there are valid reasons for
departing therefrom. In the latter case, these may
justify a statement of differences from the standard,
or the preparation of a different description, but
these should be documented, in each case, and subject
to review by internal auditors.

Detailed procedures in the Chilean Tax Service
Manual should cover the various new approaches to
personnel management, in accordance with the new laws,
and the policies approved by the Director. Analysts
should be trained, in the Office of Personnel and
Welfare and the Department of Organization and Methods,
to carry out or guide the accomplishment of these new
procedures and policies. By the end of 1966 the
benefits in improved operations, better employee morale, and lowered costs should be well apparent.
These benefits should increase each year, as further
improvements are made in the system, the personnel
become more experienced in it, and costs are reduced
since there will be fewer employees enjoying "saved
salaries" above the normal ceiling for their jobs.

APPENDIX **G** OUTLINE OF THE
PERSONNEL AND
ORGANIZATIONAL
MANAGEMENT PLAN

Basically the plan is ready for total implementation in three stages:

Stage 1: Associate the 230 job descriptions
with each unit of the Service, i.e.
describe the staffing of each unit
by number of employees; job code,
and job title (Approx. three months
work).

Stage 2: Associate the 230 job descriptions
with the workforce. This stage can
be carried out concurrently with
Stage 1 by a different group of
analysts (Approx. two months).

Stage 3: Train key personnel officers and
staff in application of the new
methods and techniques. (One month
training in Santiago).

plans are included with memorandum to the
personnel and O & M committees. The main parts of the
plan include the following:

1. A job classification system as described
in Tab A.
2. Materials in the form of 15 chapters for
the Chilean Tax Service Manual as outlined
in Tab B.

TAB A--THE CHILEAN TAX SERVICE
JOB CLASSIFICATION SYSTEM

The job classification structure shown herein
is the result of approximately eight man-years of

210

efforts by the Planning Subdivision (staff analysts
of the O & M Department) and their advisors.

The 230 job descriptions represent all technical and support jobs of the Chilean Tax Service, as
determined by a comprehensive field job analysis
survey.

For convenience of presentation, ease of understanding, and utility in day-to-day operational use,
the 230 jobs have been organized into 12 areas of
work on the basis of a high degree of similarity of
skills, knowledges and duties performed. The Areas
of Work are identified by both Codes and Grade, as
follows:

Area Code (1):	Area	Grade (2):
01	Administration	A
02	"Procesamiento"	A
03	Audit	A
04	Legal	B
05	Evaluations	C
06	Chemists	D
07	IBM	E
08	Administrative	F
09	Printing	G
10	Supplies Warehouse	H
11	Minor Services	H
12	Miscellaneous	None

(1)   All jobs classified in an Area have the
same two first digits as the Area Code. For example,
all jobs in the Administration Area have 01 as the
first two digits of the Job Code.

(2)   Grade: The alphabetical "Grade" identification will be used when there is a need to identify
the type of employee that usually qualifies for the
jobs in the Area. For example: Grade A (Inspectors)
normally will be assigned to jobs in areas 01, 02,
and 03; while Grade B (lawyers) will be limited to
area 04, and Grade D (chemists) will be limited to
area 06, etc.

The jobs in each area chart are arranged in
patterns that are significant in two aspects:

1.   There is a logic in the chart arrangement
with respect to career development. For example, a
person would normally be promoted from a job at the

bottom of the arrangement to one at the next higher
level, etc.

2.   All jobs are arranged on the chart according
to relative importance, or "Level of difficulty."
For example, jobs at the highest levels involve more
responsibility, authority, etc. than jobs at the
bottom of the chart. "Levels of Difficulty" have been
established for each job shown on the charts.

They are the result of the application of special Job Evaluation Methods which were designed to
evaluate the 230 jobs of the Service. The Levels of
Difficulty will be especially useful for career planning, determining training needs and input, and for
planning promotions, transfers and other purposes.

Training symbols are shown on the Area of Work
charts to depict the existence of, or need for certain
types of training. The various symbols used on the
charts are:

P   Practical or on-the-job training

T   Theoretical or formal classroom training

PT   Practical and Theoretical

Re
T/P   Recommended --- Training

Each job on the Area of Work chart is represented
by a rectangular box that carries three significant
bits of information about the job.

For example:

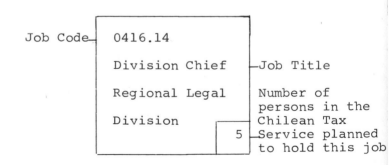

(Note: Once the system is effectuated only the Job
         Code and Job Title need be shown in the box
         representing the job.)

JOB CODES: Inspection of the attached job descrip-
             tions will reveal that each is identical
             as to format. The only aspect of the job
             description that is not self-explanatory
             is the Job Code. The Job Code is simply
             a logical "shorthand identification" for
             the job; and is commonly used on reports,
             charts, etc., with or without the Job
             Title. Users of the Job Codes will
             readily recognize the entire meaning.
             For example:

The Job Code for Chief Regional Legal Division is:

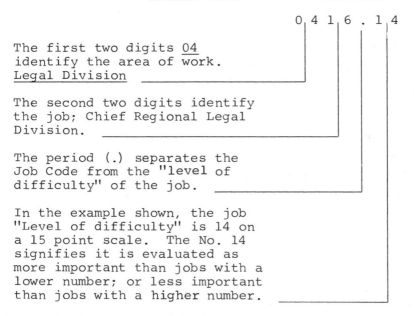

                                        0 4 1 6 . 1 4

The first two digits 04
identify the area of work.
Legal Division

The second two digits identify
the job; Chief Regional Legal
Division.

The period (.) separates the
Job Code from the "level of
difficulty" of the job.

In the example shown, the job
"Level of difficulty" is 14 on
a 15 point scale. The No. 14
signifies it is evaluated as
more important than jobs with a
lower number; or less important
than jobs with a higher number.

     An individual job incumbent who is assigned to
a job may or may not hold a pay grade that corresponds
to the "level of difficulty." As time goes on the
relationship between the job incumbant's pay grade and
the job "level of difficulty" will become generally
understood for day-to-day personnel management purposes. The relationship between pay grade and "level
of difficulty" will be more clearly defined when the
new pay grade structure has been approved by the
Congress.

All the Area of Work charts are attached; however, only a few examples of job descriptions are included as the total number (230) represent a very large
volume. Should it become necessary to inspect more
than the examples attached, they may be obtained from
the Chilean Tax Service (O & M Department).

TAB B--OUTLINE OF THE NEW
PERSONNEL MANAGEMENT SYSTEM

The purpose of submitting the attached outline of
the materials is to present a picture of the scope
of the new personnel management program covered.
There are in fact two outlines, one covering "Administration and General Organization of the Chilean Tax
Service" and the other encompassing all major areas
of the broad field of "Personnel Management."

As the primary Personnel Management Programs are
put into operation the Chilean Tax Service will be the
first governmental agency in all South America to take
the big steps forward with truly modern personnel and
organizational management systems.

As each chapter of the procedural materials were
completed they became a subject for discussions with
the Subdirector for Administration or Subdirector for
Planning, as appropriate. A joint committee composed
of representatives of each Subdirection to review the
materials and put them in the most appropriate format
before publication was established.

It does not appear that the procedural provisions
will conflict with the law, except possibly in the
areas of Employee Performance Ratings and Employee
Promotions. The greatest changes from the current
systems are in these two areas and when effectuated,
will do much to correct the problems that face the
Tax Service.

APPENDIX EVALUATION AND
CONTROL REPORTS

Work control system for Audit and Processing.
A new system of control will be effective as of
March 1 of this year with the purpose of guiding,
orienting and evaluating the audit and processing
functions. The system will operate by way of various
forms. The process will start with Form No. 1, issued at the Tax Inspectors level. It is prepared
personally by the Inspector, and serves the purpose
of, in the first place, evaluating his work and then,
by monthly comparisons, orients him as to the fulfillment of future audit plans to obtain greater efficiency in his work. At the same time this initial report
provides the Group Chief with his primary tool for
supervision.

These charts, with the exception of the ones to
be processed by the National Office, will provide the
greatest part of the information necessary to prepare
other charts for immediately higher levels of responsibility. In addition, the National Office, through
the reports received from the Zone Administration,
will prepare the information necessary for each Regional Office and Zone Office. This will be presented
in such a way so that those units of the Service may
use it to learn--on a comparative basis--the achievement against the total program for each one of the
Regional and Zone Offices throughout the country.

The system consists of 16 forms, of which the
first four will be prepared at the operative level,
from the Inspector to the Zone Administrator. Details will be provided further on. The rest of the
forms will be prepared by the National Office only
by summarizing and tabulating the data obtained in
the first four forms.

Form No. 5 is used by all levels, because it is
utilized to ask questions and to clarify data provided by all units of the Service.

215

1 (10) 11

Levels who register the data to be provided on the various forms.

(A) Inspector. The Inspector has the responsibility of reporting to his Group Chief all the audit tasks and other work assigned to him during the course of the month. This information will be provided on Form No. 1.

(B) Group Chief. He should prepare the operative report for the whole Group on Form No. 2, taking into consideration the information provided on all forms No. 1 he receives from the Audit personnel reporting to him. This includes his own supervision time report and the one corresponding to other types of work performed in the Group.

(C) Chief of Audit. He provides some processing information from the unit he is in charge of on Form No. 3. He will indicate on Form 3-A some specific details which complement the form corresponding to this responsibility. (List of taxpayers with liquidations whose income derives totally or partially from industry, trade or mining sources.)

(D) Zone Administrators. This official supervises, through the Processing Subadministrator, the preparation of the monthly and overall report for the Zone Office, on Form No. 4. The Audit and Processing data will be obtained from Forms Nos. 2 and 3 received from Group Chiefs and Chiefs of Audit of the respective jurisdiction.

(E) Regional Offices. They are exempt from preparation of control charts. Regional Offices receive from the corresponding Administrations, copy of Chart No. 4 on a monthly basis. Subsequently, from the National Office they will receive separate charts, by subject, which will provide them an overall view of the Audit and Processing activities. These charts will cover the Regional Office itself, with details of the Zone Offices, as well as the other Regional Offices in the country and their respective zones. These charts will also be sent to Zone Administrators. Charts 6 to 16 will be received monthly, by the tenth day after the close of the month, to ensure a timely reception of the information.

(F) National Office. The Statistical Department of the National Office ("Subdirección" of Planning) has the responsibility of tabulating the information received from the Administrations which reflects the overall work performance of the Service. This is accomplished on forms Nos. 6 to 16 and once it is prepared, using the work performance throughout the country, it is remitted to each Regional Office and Administration with appropriate comments.

When the data has been received on forms to be filled in at the National Office, a set of the charts containing a consolidated statement of the five Regional Offices and the 14 Zone Administrations in the country, with succinct specifications of the Audit and Processing functions, will be sent to the mentioned units on a monthly basis. In this way it is expected that Regional Directors and their advisors may duly control and direct the work performed by the units of their jurisdiction. Towards this goal, the comparison made of work performed by the other Regional Offices will be very useful, and will have an influence on the increase of the quality and quantity of work during the subsequent months.

The Audit Department of the "Subdirección" of Operations will be in charge of analyzing the charts prepared by the Statistical Department, with the purpose of making the necessary comments for each Regional Office or Administration. This Department, by means of the information gathered directly from their investigations and the charts processed by the Statistical Department, will be in a condition to effectively control the progress of the annual Audit Program in all its phases.

1(10)12

Monthly Operating Report of the Auditor. (Work Procedures for Preparation of Charts Nos. 1 to 4, Form 1(10)10-1).

This form is divided into six parts, the first three of which are prepared by the Inspector and the rest by the Supervisor, with the cooperation of the Group Chief. The design of the form permits the Inspector to use the minimum possible time to fill in the data. He also prepares two complementary forms: Nos. 3490-3 "individual control of cases, and 3490-4 or 3490-5 for control of daily hours worked, the first for Field and Office Auditors, and the second for Preventive Auditors.

This form, together with the monthly schedule of work hours (3490-4 and 3490-5) should be completed the first work day of the month that follows the one mentioned on the information, and forwarded on the same date to the Group Chief.

The amounts will be given in integral parts and, when necessary, with only one decimal. (For example, three days and four hours of work will be shown as 3,5 hs. and, even though mathematically the hour corresponds to 0,125 of the normal work day, it will be shown as 0,1 and 2 hours as 0,3, etc.). The extra hours will be expressed likewise, adding the corresponding fraction to the normal day. It should also be noted that a normal day is considered of eight work hours and Saturday, of three hours, i.e. making 43 hours for the work week. Therefore, a Saturday worked is not considered a work day, but a fraction of three hours (0,4 ds.).

The number of man-days of work performed, indicated in part I of the form, not only excludes holidays, but also the days or day-fraction during which the Tax Inspector has not been working.

1(10)12.01

Definition of "Cases":

A "case" will be considered the basic unit for audit assigned to a Field Inspector or an Office Auditor who carries out any investigation (covering 1 or more years), for corporations, partnerships and individual partnerships. When individual partnerships or corporations are involved, there is no problem in classification. Always the basic unit of a review is one individual or entity, that is, it is "a case" without distinction between corporations or individuals. Individual partnerships are covered by an audit of the corporation itself plus the total income of the partners and the taxes that may effect all the partners.

This type of audit will always be "a case" but, for the purpose of Forms 1 and 2 the number of taxpayers will be considered separately. Therefore, the Inspector who carries out the review of individual partnerships will have in his monthly report a higher number of audited taxpayers than the number of closed cases. For example, a partnership composed of 4 partners is equivalent to "a case" but counts as 5 taxpayers audited (it is recommended to Group Chiefs that the distribution of cases for audit be made on a basis that takes this system into account).

The following points regarding pending cases at the end of the month, should be very clearly stated in the Monthly Report:

(1) <u>Audit which has not yet been started</u>:
This corresponds to the number of cases which have
been assigned but on which audit has not yet been
initiated.
    (2) <u>Audit in Process</u>: This is the number of
audits which have been started but are not closed at
the time of preparing the Monthly Report.
    (3) <u>Audit in Suspense</u>: This applies to those
cases which are in suspense, with the following detail: (3A) <u>For Group Chief's Approval</u>: They are
closed cases pending the Supervisor's approval, and
(3B) <u>Other Reasons (to be specified)</u>: In this space
the Tax Inspector will indicate those cases initiated
and in suspense for other reasons, such as orders of
superior or request of the file for statistic study
purposes, or for other reasons, and which would be
returned to him when the audit is closed.

    When turning in his monthly report, the Tax In-
spector, in order to clarify his report, should discuss with the Group Chief any doubts he may have.
Similarly, the Supervisor should carefully check the
data provided by the Tax Inspector in order to reflect
reality as much as possible. The data should be received and analyzed by the Group Chief in a realistic
and objective way and with the elements of judgement
which emanate from comparisons of items on the form
itself.

    It may happen that the Tax Inspector shows too
much time spent on "other jobs." other than the audit
itself. When this happens, the Group Chief should
study the causes of the problem and try to find a solution as soon as possible, so that the auditing personnel assigned to his Group is dedicated, if possible,
exclusively to investigate tasks.

    Furthermore, if the auditor in the compilation
of cases pending at the end of the month shows as
"audit in process" a case that in reality should be
included under "audits which have not yet been started,"
the Group Official will make the necessary corrections.
Then, he should take special care to watch this item,
once the Monthly Reports processing is over, in order
that the Tax Inspector may start the audit immediately.

    In part III the Tax Inspector will indicate the
number of audited taxpayers during the month in any
type of audit. In the part corresponding to "Remarks"
in the Preventive Auditor's report, the number of
visits carried out during the month will be indicated.

Part IV, at the reverse of the form, will be destined for notes to be written by the Group Official in the following order corresponding to the first two spaces: Work days not included in part I and added to the ones really worked mentioned in that same part, will be shown as total work days of the month, plus the extra time worked during that period. In the third space the Group Chief will carefully evaluate the quality of the work and the production of his subordinates. This monthly qualification will be made known to the Tax Inspector.

Finally the Group Chief will use a final item called "Remarks" to note down other information or elements of judgement in order to facilitate the task of evaluating the report he has received.

In order to compute the time spent by the Supervisor in the tasks carried out during his monthly performance, with the total time of the Group he supervises, he should fill in Form 1(10)10-1, but only in the section that shows time.

If for very special reasons, such as Groups formed by very few Tax Inspectors, or very large geographical areas to be covered, the Group Chief assigns himself audit cases, he will control his own work on Form I. This will be done only as regards time spent in supervision and the detail of pending cases, if any. The other data, such as monthly classification and others which obviously concern him only, will not be stated. The Group Chief will limit himself to putting down the dates of preparation of the chart and his signature and he will include his own report with the rest of the file which contains the reports made by the personnel he is in charge of and used to prepare Chart 1(10)10-2.

1(10)13

Monthly Operating Report of the Audit Group Chief (Form 1(10)10-2).

The official assigned to a specific Audit Group, after the first work-day of each month and once the reports contained on Forms 1(10)10-1 are approved, will complete the data still missing in these forms. When this task is over, he will be in a condition to complete the summary of work performed by the whole Group, which includes Tax Inspectors and his own Group Chief. This is shown on Form 1(10)10-2.

Part I of the form is used to state the number of Tax Inspectors, including the Supervisor in charge of the Audit unit, who have worked during all or part of the reported month.

In part II, the man-days are noted for work performed by Tax Inspectors, including the Group Chief. This information is given by type of tax as well as by type of audit, and includes not only work performed during the audit, but also other types of work. Adding up both, we have the "total for all types of work."

Part III of the form is "Account of Cases Audited during the Month," (excluding claims), i.e. detail of inflow of cases to the Group, its development and the initial as well as final count. To the left (which is the "Debit" side of the account) it includes the inflow of cases with details explained below and to the right (the "Credit" side of the account) it includes the outflow and final count, also given in detail further on.

The "Debit" (left side) is initiated with the existing balance at the beginning of the month and should coincide with the final balance of the prior month. It includes the following:

(2) Grand total of existing cases;
    (a) Cases which have not yet been started.
    (b) Cases in process.
    (c) Cases in suspense (with subitems of points C-1, C-2 and C-3.)

Once the initial number has been consigned, the following step is:

(3) Cases assigned during the month by the Selection Office, of those received from the Selecting Committee;
(4) Cases received during the month, from other reference points;
(5) Cases transferred to other Groups;
(6) Cases received from the Tax Fraud and Internal Inspection Departments; and finally
(7) Other cases added to the count and which increase the work-load of the Group.

The "Credit" (right side) corresponds to annotations on closed cases and cases which have been left for other reasons, as well as the final detailed count, in accordance with the following:

(8) Audits closed (cases with liquidations approved in draft form by the Group Chief, either with differences or revised and approved);

(9) Cases transferred to other Groups;

(10) Potential information of tax fraud, subject to consideration of the Zone Administrator (i.e. those cases which audit was started by the Tax Inspector and submitted for the Supervisor's consideration, and which, in turn, were forwarded to the Administrator, so that he could decide if the case should be returned as contrary to regulations or should be remitted to the Tax Fraud Investigation Department).

And finally:

(11) Number of cases at the end of the month, whose detail are the same indicated for the initial number, only changing the figures.

On the reverse of the form, the total number of audited taxpayers will be noted and under the heading "Remarks" the Group Chief will add those elements of judgement he might consider necessary to clarify the data noted previously. Also under this heading, the total number of visits made by the Preventive Auditors of the Group will be indicated.

This form ends with the date and signature of the Group official who makes the report, and the date and signature of the Supervisor when he obtains the approval of the processed data, submitting it to consideration of the Chief of Zone Audit. This should be presented in original and one copy leaving a copy for the Supervisor's personal file.

This work should be completed on the fifth work day of the month following the one the information refers to.

It is recommended to Group Chiefs that before approving the data on Form 1(10)10-1, he should fill in Form 1(10)10-2, especially in relation to work performed by field and office auditors. He should then compare the information with the one contained in card "B" of Form 3490-3. This card should always be up-to-date in his files, so that the data to be summarized and processed may reflect reality in the operations of the Group he is responsible for.

1(10)14

Monthly Operating Report of the Audit Chief (Form 1(10)10-3).

The Audit Chief within the first five work days of the month following the one the information to be processed refers to, will have the personnel under his jurisdiction prepare Chart 1(10)10-3. This includes a summary of the processing work of the unit he's in charge of during the specific month, together with specific details on liquidations registered, source of origin in industry, trade or mining (Chart 1(10)10-3A), and should send them in duplicate, within the mentioned period, to the Subadministrator of Processing of the corresponding Administration.

Monthly information, tabulated by tax sources, is indicated on the same form. Number of taxpayers affected by the investigation made by Audit as a matter of routine, will be indicated on Form 1(10)10-3.

In part I of the form, notices sent during the month, with the detail of their replies, will be indicated on the form following the same order. Liquidations completed with differences of taxes and claims against liquidations presented by taxpayers during the month, will also be provided. Details of this information are as follows:

(A)   Returns received from Non-Filers on the Tax Rolls: In the first place, the number of notices sent by the Audit during the month, which will correspond to taxpayers who failed to file their returns on time, are indicated. Then comes the number of responses received during the month, disregarding the month during which the notices or summonses were sent. The responses received have been subdivided into number of returns received, or reasons for which the notified or summoned taxpayers failed to file, [point 2 which includes (A), (B) and (C)].

Ten-day notices sent to taxpayers during the month and which will only be noted as number of taxpayers in point 3, will correspond to those notifications used by the Inspection to clarify the data related to their returns or other matters connected with petitions. The boxes crossed out with XXX on the form indicate that the corresponding information is not needed for the time being.

(B) Taxpayers who have received Notices on
Differences: In points 4 and 5 with their corresponding subdivisions, the Audit Chief indicates the number
of taxpayers who have received notices due to increased assessments in taxes and the Escudo value of
these assessments.

As it is determined in the Tax Code, the total
amount of the liquidations will be stated in the
corresponding boxes, i.e. the taxes as they are noted
plus the surcharges by special laws, sanctions, fines
and interests derived from the assessment.

Point 4-A, which derives from point 4, (specific
details given on form 1(10)10-3A), only indicates the
number of taxpayers whose liquidations with differences, emanate totally or partially from trade, industry or mining.

For statistical study purposes, a special tabulation is required for point 5, i.e. the total amount
of the value of liquidations, subdivided by those
values corresponding to the year of selection, and
the amount of the differences from previous years.
These amounts will be tabulated as indicated in the
book of Registered Liquidations which will be used
country-wide.

(C) Taxpayer's Claims against Liquidations (1st.
Instance): Even when the workload for claims against
tax liquidations corresponds to Audit (because of the
reports emanating from their Tax Inspectors) the Inspection (Small Processing Office) should report in
this part of the form, the detail of the claims,
their initial number and also the ones resolved during
the month, and the final count.

In the first place, point 6 corresponds to claims
pending at the beginning of the month: detail should
be given covering claims in Audit and then sent for
handling at the Zone or Region (point 6A and 6B).
Then, in point 7, claims received by Audit during the
month are indicated, either the ones presented directly
by those affected by it, or those received from other
units: (Zone or Regional Offices) and which should be
reported by the personnel assigned to Audit.

As regards resolved claims, the Audit Chief will
report in detail on such resolutions, as claims may
have been resolved completely favorable to the taxpayer, a partial reduction of the amount involved may

have been obtained, or else the Administration or Regional Office (depending on the amount involved) may have resolved on the complete rejection of the claim. Points 8 to 14 give this data in detail indicating in the first place the number of claims resolved and then, the amount of taxes and surcharges which have been accepted, rejected or partially accepted. Finally, information on final number of claims is provided, in the audit function as well as in the respective Administrations or Regional Offices.

In part II of the form, the Inspector makes a recount of the flow of claims received, processed and pending during the month, with the number of claimants and source of the taxes referred to in the claims. This excludes liquidations claims.

The Audit Chief also has a space where he can make any "Remarks" to clarify points which he personally considers should be made clear. He submits the form with his signature and the date on which the process of information is closed, to the consideration of the Administration on the 5th. work-day of the month, in duplicate, and attaches 2 copies of Chart 1(10)10-3A.

1(10)14.01

Supplement to the Monthly Report of the Audit Chief (Chart 1(10)10-3A).

It is requested that this form be filled in with detail of the liquidations processed during the month which are connected with tax differences derived totally or partially from Industry, Trade or Mining. This is to permit the National Office to obtain timely information from the very source of origin.

Apart from individualizing the case, the symbol of the economic activity should be indicated, together with the last Capital and Reserve of the taxpayer. This data should be given on the respective liquidations. Thus also the Group Chiefs should be instructed so they can ask the same from the Inspectors. If this data is not indicated in the respective liquidations, the Chief of Inspection should obtain it from the files.

This form is made out in triplicate in order to send two copies together with Form 1(10)10-3 to Administration, and permit the Audit Chief to keep one for his files.

1(10)15

Monthly Operating Report of the Zone Administrator - (Form 1(10)10-4).

Once all Forms 1(10)10-2 from Audit Groups and
Forms 1(10)10-2 from jurisdictional Audits, are received, the Processing Subadministrator with the cooperation of the Statistical Zone Office proceeds to
consolidate the information for audit and processing.
This is done on Form 1(10)10-4 and submitted for the
approval of the Zone Administrator. Once approved
by him, together with copies of Form 1(10)10-3A from
Audit, it is sent in two copies to the National Office Audit Department and to the Statistical Department. This should be done at the latest on the 15th.
of the month following the one the information refers
to. The Administrator keeps a copy for the Administration files and sends another copy to the Regional
Director.

In part I of the form, the Zone Administration
gives the data which corresponds to the progressive
development point of the annual audit program approved
by National Offices, for the respective administration.

Parts II, III, IV, V and VI correspond to totals
of audit information which will be summarized from
the different forms 1(10)10-2 received from Audit
Groups through the Chief of Zone Audit.

Parts VII and VIII, correspond to the summary of
the processing procedures from all Audits which depend from the reporting Administration.

In part IX the Zone Administration indicates
transfers to and from the Tax Fraud Investigation
Department occurred during the month.

In part X, and as an advance of the compilation
of audit information, the Administration will consider
from an arithmetical viewpoint the relationship of
time spent by the Zone Auditors in the auditing itself; the number of man-months in Audit; and finally
the total differences by man-month in Audit. To the
right margin of part X there is a space for remarks
which the Administrator may note down and which permits clarification of the processed information.

Finally, at the reverse of the second page of
the form, the date of approval and dispatch by the

Administrator, and the summary of information for his zone is indicated. This is sent together with Forms 1(10)10-3A corresponding to Audit to the National Office, as well as to the corresponding Regional Office.

1(10)16

Questions concerning an Operating Report - Form 1(10)10-5.

If an official of any of the levels responsible for the issuance of monthly information has any doubts in relation to data given on the respective charts, he must contact the office or Group who issued the information, in order that they reply on the same form. This avoids errors in the interpretation of the question and facilitates the internal medium of communication related to the statistical information system.

The fact of an answer not being received in time by the office that raises the question will not delay the preparation of forms within the established target date. According to the importance of the error, if it is not considered during the month in question, a corresponding remark will be made on the following month to the respective chart.

1(10)17

Forms Nos. 6 to 16 prepared by the Statistical Department.

With the data assembled from all units and obtained on forms 1(10)10-4 made by the 14 Zone Administrations in the country, the Statistical Department of the "Subdirección" of Studies, will tabulate the information and will prepare a set of forms which will include all the audit and processing procedures used throughout the country. Detail of these forms is given below:

Form 1(10)10-6:   Audit and available personnel program during the Audit.

Form 1(10)10-7:   Man-months of work performed during the Audit.

Form 1(10)10-8:   Work performed in the obtention of returns.

Form 1(10)10-9:   Debits in the audited cases Account.

Form 1(10)10-10:   Credits in the Audited Cases
                   Account and other information.
Form 1(10)10-11:   Taxpayers who have received
                   notice on differances.
Form 1(10)10-12:   Value of liquidations through
                   tax sources.
Form 1(10)10-13:   Amount of the differences
                   which derive totally or par-
                   tially from industry, trade
                   and/or mining.
Form 1(10)10-14:   Number of claims resolved and
                   pending.
Form 1(10)10-15:   Amount of accepted claims.
Form 1(10)10-16:   Claims in Audit, excluding the
                   ones referred to liquidations.

The complete set of the above forms, which will
carry country-wide data by Regional Offices and Administrations, will be passed on to the offices by
the Statistical Department, on a monthly basis, during
the course of the month next to the one that information refers to. In this way, Regional Directors and
Zone Administrators are ensured a timely reception
of the data. By comparing the different operative
units within the country, they may determine their
relationship within its geographic-economic potential.
Also it will provide information for the control of
the Chiefs responsible for the work in order to
achieve success in achieving the established goals.

CHART 1(10)10-1

Monthly Operating Report of the Auditor

Region_____

Zone Number_____Audit_____

Group Number_____Year_____Month of Operation_____

Name of Auditor_____

I

MAN-DAYS OF WORK PERFORMED

1. - Total for all kinds of operation_ _

TIME IN AUDITING BY SOURCE OF TAX			TYPES OF AUDITING				
	Field	Office	Preventive				Grand Total
			General	Special	Extraord.	Total	
	(a)	(b)	(c)	(d)	(e)	(f)	(g)
2. Income							
3. Buying and Selling							
4. Turnover							
5. Acts and Contracts							
6. Alcohol and Alcoholic Beverages							
7. Others (to be specified)							
8. Totals							
9. Time in reporting claims resulting from liquidations							

10. Time on training

11. Time on Selection Committee

12. Time on supervision, review and other operations (to be specified)

Grand Total

IV | WORK-DAYS NOT INCLUDED IN PART I

1. Permission------------_____   4. Temporary duty----------_____

2. Holiday----------------_____   5. Late arrival------------_____

3. Leave------------------_____   6. Others------------------_____
                                              (to be specified)

Acceptance of this report by the Group Chief
(not to be applied to his own report)

Day_____Month_____Year_____ _____
                                                 Signature of the Group Chief

---

EVALUATION AND BASIS

	Quality	Yield
1. Very Good	☐	☐
2. Good	☐	☐
3. Fair	☐	☐
4. Less than fair	☐	☐
5. Poor	☐	☐

(Yield in relation with the standard of cases)

REMARKS

230

II | WORKLOAD AT END OF MONTH

    1. Audits not started-------------------------------------_____

    2. Audits in process------------------------------------_____

    3. Audits pending---------------------------------------_____

    3-A. Audits for approval of the Group Chief--------------_____

    3-B. Other reasons (to be specified)-----------_____

              ----

    4. Total of cases pending-------------------------------_____

II | TOTAL OF TAXPAYERS AUDITED---------------------------------_____

REMARKS

Submission of this report to the Group Chief
(or completion by the Group Chief of his own
report)

Day_____Month_____Year_____

                                           Signature of the Auditor

231

CHART 1(10)10-2

Monthly Operating Report of the Audit Group Chief

Region_____

Zone Number_____

Group Number_____Year_____Month of Operation_____

Name of Group Chief_____

I | NUMBER OF AUDITORS, INCLUDING THE GROUP CHIEF_____
(assigned during all or part of the month)

II | MAN-DAYS OF WORK PERFORMED BY THE AUDITORS, INCLUDING THE GROUP CHIEF
1. Total for all kinds of operation_ _ _ _ _ _ _ _ _ _ _ _ _ _ _____

TIME IN AUDITING BY SOURCE OF TAX	TYPES OF AUDITING						
	Field	Office	Preventive				Grand
			General	Special	Extraord.	Total	Total
	(a)	(b)	(c)	(d)	(e)	(f)	(g)
2. Income							
3. Buying and Selling							
4. Turnover							
5. Acts and Contracts							
6. Alcohol and Alcoholic Beverages							
7. Others (to be specified)							
8. Totals							
9. Time in reporting claims resulting from liquidations							
10. Time on training							___
11. Time on Selection Committee							___
12. Time on supervision, review and other operations (to be specified)							___
						Grand Total	

232

III | CASES AUDITED DURING THE MONTH (excluding claims)

1. Total number of cases included in
   the workload at any time of the
   month.._____

2. Workload at beginning of
   month, grand total......._____

2-A. Audits not started_____

2-B. Audits in process_____

2-C. Audits pending_____

2-C-1. To be approved by the
       Group Chief_____

2-C-2. Potential information
       on tax frauds to be
       reviewed by the
       Group Chief.........._____

2-C-3. Other reasons........_____

3. Cases assigned pursuant
   to selection by the
   Committee.............._____

4. Cases received from other
   other reference
   points................._____

   (.......Number of Taxpayers)

5. Transferred from other
   Groups................._____

6. Returned by Intelligence
   Department or Zone....._____

7. Other additions to
   workload..............._____

   (to be specified)..............
   ....

8. Audit completed
   (liquidation approved_____

8-A. Examined without
     showing differences_____

8-B. Transmitted to
     Processing because
     of differences
     shown.............._____

9. Transferred to other
   Groups.............._____

10. Potential information
    transferred to the
    Zone Administrator_____

11. Others (to be
    specified)........_____
    ....

12. Workload at end of
    month............_____ _____

12-A. Audit not started_____

12-B. Audit in process_____

12-C. Audit pending_____

12-C-1. To be approved
        by the Group
        Chief_____

12-C-2. Potential Infor-
        mation on tax frauds to
        to be reviewed
        by the Group Chief_____

12-C-3. Others............_____
        (to be specified)
        ....

```
TOTAL OF TAXPAYERS AUDITED.................................._____
```

```
REMARKS
```

```
Submission of this              Approval of this
report to the Group             report by the Group
Chief or Group Clerk            Chief and submission
                                in duplicate to the
                                Zonal Chief of Audit


Day____Month_____Year_____  Day____Month_____Year



    _____              _____
    Signature of Clerk               Signature of Group Chief
```

234

CHART 1(10)10-3

Monthly Operating Report of the Office Chief

Region_____Zone Number_____Month_____

Audit_____Month_____

Name of Office Chief_____

RETURNS, LIQUIDATIONS AND CLAIMS PROCESSED	Total of Tax-Payers (a)	SOURCES OF TAX						
		Income (b)	Buying and Selling (c)	Real Estate (d)	Turn-over (e)	Acts and Contracts (f)	Alcohols etc. (g)	Other (h)
1. Notices sent to nonfilers on the tax rolls								
2. Total of responses during the month to notices and summonses sent, regardless of the month during which the notices were sent								
2-A. Number of returns received..........								
REASONS FOR NON-FILING								
2-B. Return filed else-where								
2-C. Tax liability terminated								
2-D. Other (to be summarized under "Remarks")								
3. Ten-day notices sent to taxpayers		XXX	XXX	XXX	XXX	XXX	XXX	XXX
TAXPAYERS WHO HAVE RECEIVED NOTICES OF DIFFERENCES SHOWN								
4. Taxpayers with liqui-dations completed		XXX	XXX	XXX	XXX	XXX	XXX	XXX
4-A. Taxpayers with liquidations showing differences based wholly or in part on trade, industry or mining (for more de-tails see Form 1(10)10-3A)		XXX	XXX	XXX	XXX	XXX	XXX	XXX

235

II | F L O W   O F   P E T I T I O N S

DETAIL	Total of Petitions (a)	SOURCES OF TAX						
		Income (b)	Buying and Selling (c)	Real Estate (d)	Turn-over (e)	Acts and Contracts (f)	Alcohols etc. (g)	Other (h)
Number of petitions (excluding those on claims resulting from liquidations) 1. Pending at beginning of month 2. Received 3. Allowed 4. Pending at end of month								

REMARKS

Submission of this report
to the Zone Processing
Subadministrator

Signature of Office Chief
(including Zone Headquarters
Office)

Day_____Month_____Year_____

5. Amount of all liquidations	XXX	E°	E°	XXX	E°	E°	E°	E°
5A. Based on year of selection	XXX	E°	E°	XXX	E°	E°	E°	E°
5B. Based on previous years	XXX	E°	E°	XXX	E°	E°	E°	E°

TAXPAYERS' CLAIMS AGAINST LIQUIDATIONS

6. Pending at the beginning of the month		XXX	XXX	XXX	XXX	XXX	XXX	XXX
6A. Number of Audit		XXX	XXX	XXX	XXX	XXX	XXX	XXX
6B. Zone or Region Number		XXX	XXX	XXX	XXX	XXX	XXX	XXX
7. Received during the month		XXX	XXX	XXX	XXX	XXX	XXX	XXX

CLAIMS ALLOWED IN FULL

8. Number of Claims		XXX	XXX	XXX	XXX	XXX	XXX	XXX
9. Amounts allowed (taxes)	XXX	E°	E°	XXX	E°	E°	E°	E°

CLAIMS ALLOWED IN PART

10. Number of Claims		XXX	XXX	XXX	XXX	XXX	XXX	XXX
11. Amounts allowed (taxes)	XXX	E°	E°	XXX	E°	E°	E°	E°
12. Total amounts claimed (taxes)	XXX	E°	E°	XXX	E°	E°	E°	E°

CLAIMS REJECTED IN FULL

13. Number of Claims		XXX	XXX	XXX	XXX	XXX	XXX	XXX
14. Amounts claimed (taxes)	XXX	E°	E°	XXX	E°	E°	E°	E°

PENDING AT END OF MONTH

15. Number of Claims	XXX	XXX	XXX	XXX	XXX	XXX	XXX	XXX
15A. Number in printing	XXX	XXX	XXX	XXX	XXX	XXX	XXX	XXX
15B. Number in Zone or Region	XXX	XXX	XXX	XXX	XXX	XXX	XXX	XXX

CHART 1(10)10-3 A

Supplement to the Monthly Operating
Report of the Office Chief

Region_____Zone Number_____Year_____

Audit_____Month_____

Name of Office Chief_____

LIQUIDATIONS SHOWING DIFFERENCES BASED WHOLLY OR IN PART ON TRADE, INDUSTRY OR MINING.			
TAXPAYER NAME AND ADDRESS	Symbol of Economic Activity	Capital and Reserves (Escudos)	Total Amount of Liquidations

Submission of this report in duplicate
to the Zone Processing Subadministrator

Day_____Month_____Year_____

_____
Signature of Office Chief
(including Zone Headquarters
Office)

238

CHART 1(10)10-4

Monthly Operating Report of the Zone Administrator

Region_____ _____Zone Number_____Year_____

Name of Administrator_____

Month of Operation_____

I	ANNUAL AUDIT PROGRAM

ANNUAL AUDIT PROGRAM
1. Total number of cases selected by the Committee for the annual audit program
2. Total of cases assigned to date (Part III, Nos. 3 and 4 of Form 1(10)10-2) plus those included in previous months
3. Balance of cases to be assigned for the rest of the program

II NUMBER OF OFFICIAL WORKDAYS IN THE ZONE DURING THE MONTH _ _ _ _ _ _ _ _ _

III NUMBER OF AUDITORS INCLUDING GROUP CHIEFS ASSIGNED DURING ALL OR PART OF THE MONTH _ _ _ _ _ _ _ _ _ _ _ _ _ _ _ _ _ _ _

IV MAN-DAYS OF WORK PERFORMED BY AUDITORS, INCLUDING GROUP CHIEFS

1. Total for all kinds of operation _ _ _ _ _ _ _ _ _ _ _ _ _ _ _ _ _ _ _

TIME IN AUDITING BY SOURCE OF TAX	Field (a)	Office (b)	TYPES OF AUDITING				Grand Total (g)
			Preventive				
			General (c)	Special (d)	Extraord. (e)	Total (f)	
2. Income							
3. Buying and Selling							
4. Turnover							
5. Acts and Contracts Contracts							
6. Alcohol and Alcoholic Beverages							
7. Others (to be specified)							
8. Totals							
9. Time in reporting claims resulting from liquidations							

239

10. Time on training _

11. Time on Selection Committee _

12. Time on supervision, review and other operations _ _ _ _ _ _ _ _ _ _ _ _ _
    (to be specified)

	Grand Total

V ACCOUNT OF CASES AUDITED AND NUMBER OF TAXPAYERS (excluding claims)

1. Total number of cases assigned any time during the month - - - - - _____

2. Workload at beginning of month, grand total---------------_____	8. Audit completed (liquidations approved) -----------------_____
2-A. Audits not started-------_____	8-A. Examined without showing differences--------------_____
2-B. Audits in process--------_____	
2-C. Audits pending-----------_____	8-B. Transmitted to Processing because of differences shown--------------------_____
2-C-1. To be approved by the Group Chief-----------_____	9. Transferred to other groups--------------------_____
2-C-2. Potential Information on tax frauds to be reviewed by the Group Chief------_____	10. Potential information transferred to the Zone Administrator--------------------_____
2-C-3. Other reasons-----------_____	11. Other (to be specified)---_____
3. Cases assigned pursuant to selection by the Committee_____	12. Workload at end of month--_____
4. Cases received from other reference points (..... number of taxpayers)------_____	12-A. Audits not started------_____
	12-B. Audits in process------_____
5. Transferred from other groups--------------------_____	12-C. Audits pending---------_____
6. Returned by Intelligence Department or Zone--------_____	12-C-1. To be approved by the Group Chief----------_____
7. Other additions to workload (to be specified)---------_____	12-C-2. Potential Information on tax frauds to be reviewed by the Group Chief----------------_____
	12-C-3. Other reasons (to be specified)-----------_____

VI	TOTAL OF TAXPAYERS AUDITED---

VII FLOW OF PETITIONS

Detail	Total of Petitions (a)	Income (b)	Buying and Selling (c)	Real Estate (d)	Turn-over (e)	Acts and Contracts (f)	Alcohols Alc.Bev. (g)	Other Taxes (h)
Number of Petitions (excluding those on claims resulting from liquidations)								
1. Pending at beginning of month----------								
2. Received-------								
3. Allowed--------								
4. Pending at end of month-------								

VIII RETURNS, LIQUIDATIONS AND CLAIMS PROCESSED

Detail	Total of tax-payers (a)	Income (b)	Buying and Selling (c)	Real Estate (d)	Turn-over (e)	Acts and Contracts (f)	Alcohols Alc.Bev. (g)	Other Taxes (h)
1. Notices and summons sent to non-filers on the tax roll--------								
2. Responses during the month, regardless of the month during which the notices were sent. Total----------								
2.A Number of returns received- REASONS FOR NON-FILING								
2.B Returns filed elsewhere								

241

2.C Liability Terminated--------								
2.D Other (to be summarized under "Remarks)								
3. Ten-day notices sent to tax-payers---------		XXX	XXX	XXX	XXX	XXX	XXX	XXX
TAXPAYERS WHO HAVE RECEIVED NOTICES ON DIFFERENCES SHOWN								
4. Taxpayers with liquidations completed		XXX	XXX	XXX	XXX	XXX	XXX	XXX
4.A Taxpayers with liquidations showing differences based wholly or in part on trade, industry or mining (for more details see Form 1(10)10-3A----		XXX	XXX	XXX	XXX	XXX	XXX	XXX
5. Amount of all liquidations---	XXX	E^O	E^O	XXX	E^O	E^O	E^O	E^O
5.A Based on year of selection	XXX	E^O	E^O	XXX	E^O	E^O	E^O	E^O
5.B Based on previous year----	XXX	E^O	E^O	XXX	E^O	E^O	E^O	E^O
TAXPAYERS' CLAIMS AGAINST LIQUIDATIONS								
6. Pending at beginning of month-----------		XXX	XXX	XXX	XXX	XXX	XXX	XXX
6.A Number of Audit		XXX	XXX	XXX	XXX	XXX	XXX	XXX
6.B Zone or Region number		XXX	XXX	XXX	XXX	XXX	XXX	XXX
7. Received during the month------		XXX	XXX	XXX	XXX	XXX	XXX	XXX
CLAIMS ALLOWED IN FULL								
8. Number of claims		XXX	XXX	XXX	XXX	XXX	XXX	XXX
9. Amounts allowed (taxes)	XXX	E^O	E^O	XXX	E^O	E^O	E^O	E^O

CLAIMS ALLOWED IN PART								
10. Number of claims		XXX	XXX	XXX	XXX	XXX	XXX	XXX
11. Amounts allowed (taxes)	XXX	E^O	E^O	XXX	E^O	E^O	E^O	E^O
12. Total amounts claimed (taxes)	XXX	E^O	E^O	XXX	E^O	E^O	E^O	E^O
CLAIMS REJECTED IN FULL								
13. Number of claims		XXX	XXX	XXX	XXX	XXX	XXX	XXX
14. Amount of claims (taxes)	XXX	E^O	E^O	XXX	E^O	E^O	E^O	E^O
PENDING AT END OF MONTH								
15. Number of claims		XXX	XXX	XXX	XXX	XXX	XXX	XXX
15.A Number of audit		XXX	XXX	XXX	XXX	XXX	XXX	XXX
15.B Zone or Region number		XXX	XXX	XXX	XXX	XXX	XXX	XXX

IX   TRANSFER TO AND FROM INTELLIGENCE DEPARTMENT

1.   Information submitted to Intelligence Department (workload) -----------

2.   Rejected information received through Regional Office (workload) ------

---

X   PRINCIPAL RELATIONSHIPS   REMARKS

1. Percent of auditor man-days spent in auditing------------%

2. Number of man-months in auditing (total man-days in auditing divided by the number of official workdays)____

3. Total of differences per man-month in auditing--------E^O____

Submission of this report and transmission of copies each to the National Office and the Regional Office

Day_____Month_____Year_____   Signature of Zone Administrator

ABOUT THE AUTHOR

Norman D. Nowak is Director of a Tax Advisory
team that for the past three years has been working
with the Government of Argentina to reorganize and
reconstructure the country's tax administration.
Previously, he was involved in similar work in Chile.

His prior experience includes twelve years as
Assistant Regional Commissioner of the Internal Revenue Services in the New York Region and several
years as Adjunct Professor at New York University's
Graduate School of Public Administration. The author
of numerous articles on tax and tax administration,
Mr. Nowak has done a considerable amount of consulting
in this field.